Transmute Your Mindset And Your Behind Will Follow

Cultivate Your Mind to Eliminate Self-Defeating Thoughts, Negative Behavior and Feelings of Being Stuck

Ree Lay Storey

Copyright © 2024 Ree Lay Storey. All rights reserved.

The content within this book may not be reproduced, duplicated, or transmitted without direct written permission from the author or the publisher.

Under no circumstances will any blame or legal responsibility be held against the publisher, or author, for any damages, reparation, or monetary loss due to the information contained within this book, either directly or indirectly.

Legal Notice:

This book is copyright protected. It is only for personal use. You cannot amend, distribute, sell, use, quote, or paraphrase any part of the content within this book, without the consent of the author or publisher.

Disclaimer Notice:

Please note the information contained within this document is for educational and entertainment purposes only. All effort has been expended to present accurate, up-to-date, reliable, and complete information. No warranties of any kind are declared or implied. Readers acknowledge that the author is not engaged in the rendering of legal, financial, medical, or professional advice. The content within this book has been derived from various sources. Please consult a licensed professional before attempting any techniques outlined in this book.

By reading this document, the reader agrees that under no circumstances is the author responsible for any losses, direct or indirect, that are incurred as a result of the use of the information contained within this document, including, but not limited to, errors, omissions, or inaccuracies.

"When you change the way you look at things, the things you look at change."

— Wayne Dyer

Contents

Introduction ... 9

Part 1
Understanding Mindset

1. THE DEPTHS OF MINDSET ... 17
   - What Is a Mindset? ... 19
   - Examples of Mindset ... 22
   - How Mindset Is Formed ... 24
   - The Impact of Mindset ... 25
   - Is Mindset Changeable? ... 27
   - Summary ... 32
   - Conclusion ... 33

Part 2
Patterns Holding You Back from Progress

2. BREAKING THE CHAINS OF LIMITING BELIEFS ... 37
   - What Are Limiting Beliefs? ... 38
   - The Impact of Limiting Beliefs ... 42
   - Identifying Your Limiting Beliefs ... 44
   - Changing Self-Talk ... 47
   - Summary ... 52
   - Conclusion ... 53

3. BREAKING THE CYCLE OF NEGATIVE THINKING ... 55
   - What Are Negative Thinking Patterns? ... 57
   - Common Negative Thinking Patterns ... 61
   - Cognitive Restructuring ... 65
   - Thought Records ... 67
   - Summary ... 70
   - Conclusion ... 71

4. CONQUERING YOUR FEARS 73
   Understanding Fear 75
   Fear of Failure 77
   Fear of Success 78
   Fear of Rejection 80
   Reframing Fear as Opportunity 81
   Managing Your Fear in the Moment 85
   Summary 87
   Conclusion 88

5. ESCAPING THE GRIP OF SELF-SABOTAGE 91
   Understanding Self-Sabotage 93
   Common Self-Sabotaging Behaviors 97
   Nurturing Self-Compassion 102
   Summary 107
   Conclusion 108

Part 3
Nurturing a Mindset for Success

6. CULTIVATING A GROWTH MINDSET 111
   Why Growth Mindset Matters 112
   The Consequences of Fixed Mindset Patterns 115
   Fixed Mindset and Imposter Syndrome 117
   Tips for Cultivating a Growth Mindset 120
   Summary 121
   Conclusion 123

7. THE POWER OF SELF-AWARENESS 125
   Understanding Self-Awareness 126
   Impact of Self-Awareness 128
   Mindfulness 132
   Incorporating Mindfulness into Daily Life 139
   Journaling 141
   Seeking Feedback 144
   Summary 150
   Conclusion 152

Part 4
Sustaining Positive Changes

8. ADDITIONAL STRATEGIES FOR LASTING SUCCESS	155
Engaging in Self-Care	156
Surrounding Yourself with Support	163
Setting Personal Goals	166
Tracking Progress and Celebrating Success	169
Summary	171
Conclusion	172
Conclusion	175
References	189

Introduction

 "What lies behind us and what lies ahead of us are tiny matters compared to what lives within us."

— Henry Stanley Haskins

For a long time, I was in a relationship that just wasn't working anymore. It felt like we were stuck in a loop of misunderstandings and frustrations. I kept holding onto hope, thinking that things would get better if we just tried harder. I was scared to let go because I thought it meant I had failed.

The moment everything started to change was when I realized that being in this relationship was like trying to fit a square peg into a round hole. No matter how much we tried to change or adapt, we just weren't right for each other. This realization was scary but also kind of freeing. I saw that staying in this relationship, hoping it would somehow work out, was holding me back from growing and finding happiness elsewhere.

Once I accepted that it was okay to let go, my whole perspective shifted. I started to see the end of the relationship not as a failure but as a step toward a happier, healthier life. It wasn't easy and took some time, but gradually, I began to see opportunities for growth instead of barriers. I learned a lot about myself, about what I really need and want from a partner, and how to communicate better.

This change didn't happen overnight. It came from taking small steps, like spending more time on my hobbies, reconnecting with friends, and eventually being open to meeting new people. Each step reinforced my belief that I could move on and find joy again.

Looking back, this journey taught me a lot about the power of adopting a growth mindset in relationships. I learned that sometimes, letting go of something that isn't working is the best way to open up space for new growth. I discovered a resilience in myself and a capacity to adapt and thrive that I hadn't known before. This experience showed me that our greatest potential often lies just on the other side of a tough decision, in our ability to grow, change, and move forward, even when it's hard.

So, I am not just someone who researched and wrote about these topics—I have lived through them, learned from them, and came out stronger on the other side. These theories and tactics have worked for me and others I've helped. My experience of letting go, growing, and ultimately thriving underscores that the greatest transformations and achievements are not determined by our external circumstances but by the strength, resilience, and potential that reside within us.

I wrote this book for others who feel like they're stuck. You might have trouble setting clear goals or feel like you're not achieving what you're capable of. Maybe you procrastinate, doubt yourself, or feel like you can't make the changes you want in your life. It's not uncommon to feel this way, and it's what brings many people to seek help: You've reached a point where you're ready to change but aren't sure how.

If you're seeking ways to enhance your life, this guide is for you. It offers practical strategies for individuals ready to invest effort into creating their desired future. I am proof that if you change your mindset, you can overcome the challenges hindering you.

We'll start by learning to recognize and shift your mindset, then move on to identifying and overcoming obstacles. Finally, we'll discuss how to maintain positive change. Throughout, we'll explain why it's hard to feel good about yourself and how negative thinking patterns can trap you. We'll address distorted thinking and poor coping skills that hinder your ability to see opportunities. Additionally, we'll explore broader influences like technology and economic stress, showing how they can make you feel stuck. My goal is to equip you with the tools to move past self-defeating behaviors and reach your true potential.

The methods you'll learn include:

- Using reflective prompts to guide introspection
- Practicing positive self-talk for a healthier mindset

- Implementing cognitive restructuring to change unhelpful thought patterns
- Creating a thought record to identify and adjust responses to stress
- Developing self-compassion to treat yourself with kindness
- Applying mindfulness to remain present and reduce anxiety
- Learning how to ask for and provide constructive feedback
- Utilizing self-care strategies to maintain mental and emotional well-being
- Building a supportive network to help you through tough times
- Setting SMART goals for clear, achievable objectives
- Keeping track of your progress and celebrating every victory, big or small

By the end, you'll clearly understand your challenges and a path to overcoming them, opening the door to a more fulfilled and confident life.

As you apply the methods from this book, remember that the key to a better life is not altering the external world but tapping into and cultivating the vast potential within yourself. By shifting your mindset, releasing what no longer benefits you, and embracing growth, you can achieve a happier and healthier life, demonstrating the immense power you hold within.

We'll start by learning how to change how you think. Next, we'll look at how to face problems and keep making positive changes. We'll explore why it's tough to stay positive and how negative thoughts can stop you. We'll also discuss the wrong ways of thinking and the bad ways to deal with problems, including how stress from things like technology and money affects us. This is the beginning of moving toward a happier and more satisfying life.

Part 1
Understanding Mindset

Chapter 1
The Depths of Mindset

Two friends, Alex and Jamie, face a pivotal moment together. After receiving job rejection emails from a company they were both eager to join, their reactions differ significantly.

Alex's reaction to the job rejection is deep and visceral, a moment where all the enthusiasm and dreams seem to hit a wall. As he sinks further into his chair, it feels like a metaphorical descent into a whirlpool of self-doubt and introspection. The rejection email, a mere collection of words on a screen, feels like a heavy verdict on his capabilities and choices. "Perhaps this industry isn't right for me," he quietly concludes, feeling defeated by the rejection.

Jamie, unlike Alex, doesn't let the job rejection emails deflate his spirits. Instead of sinking into self-doubt, Jamie leans back, takes a deep breath, and sees the rejection not as a defeat but a challenge. "This is just a stepping stone," Jamie thinks, an opportunity to grow and sharpen his skills. He believes that setbacks are not a reflection of his worth or capabilities but a part of the journey to success. "What can I learn from this? How can I improve?" Jamie muses, already thinking about the next opportunity.

How will these contrasting mindsets shape their paths in the days to follow? Will Alex remain in the shadow of rejection, or will he begin to see challenges as opportunities for growth? And how will Jamie's resilient attitude pave the way for future successes?

As we delve into the intricacies of mindset, we'll explore the profound impact our beliefs and attitudes have on our lives. From the way we confront academic hurdles, navigate the complexities of relationships, and advance in our careers to how we maintain our health and well-being and pursue personal growth, our mindset is the lens through which we interpret our world.

This scenario exemplifies what we'll unravel in this chapter: the power of mindset. Whether fixed or growth, our mindset influences our immediate reactions and sets the stage for our long-term achievements and fulfillment. Through understanding and potentially reshaping our mindset, the true artist of our reality is none other than ourselves. How, then, can we cultivate a mindset that serves us and propels us forward? Discover how your deepest beliefs shape your reality and how, by altering these beliefs, we can transform our lives.

What Is a Mindset?

There is power to our thoughts, and they work to shape our reality. One way to think about your mind is as an artist, constantly shaping and reshaping your world with the clay of beliefs. This artist chooses between two distinct types: the fixed mindset clay, which is somewhat rigid and hard to mold, and the growth mindset clay, which is flexible, adaptable, and ready to be shaped into anything you desire. Your mindset, this set of beliefs about yourself and the world, is the lens through which you see life, influencing how you think, feel, and act in various situations (Cherry, 2022).

People with a fixed mindset believe their abilities are carved in stone, unchangeable, like a hardened sculpture that cannot be modified. They think talent alone leads to success, overlooking the power of effort. Taking this view can lead to habitually avoiding challenges, fearing failure, and feeling threatened by others' success because you're more focused on proving you're smart or talented than becoming better (Meier, n.d.).

The opposing view is believing that your talents and abilities are like clay, malleable, and able to evolve through effort, persistence, and learning. It's the idea that you can improve your basic qualities through dedication and work. This mindset fosters a love for learning, resilience in the face of setbacks, and the understanding that effort is the path to mastery. It's also called having a growth mindset (Davis, n.d.).

The implications of your mindset are profound. A growth mindset leads to a hunger for learning and resilience, which is essential for great achievement. It makes you open to feedback, willing to take on challenges, and persistent in the face of obstacles. The focus is on your journey toward becoming better, not just proving how good you are compared to others.

Your mindset influences everything from your relationship with failure to your willingness to step out of your comfort zone. It shapes how you approach your goals, interact with others, and interpret your abilities. We know that mindsets are not set in stone. With awareness and effort, you can shift from a fixed to a growth mindset and open up a new network of possibilities for growth.

Mindset, Attitudes, and Beliefs

Mindset, attitudes, and beliefs are interconnected facets of our psychological makeup that influence how we perceive and interact with the world.

- **Mindset** is the comprehensive set of attitudes and beliefs we have about ourselves and the world around us. It's our mental inclination or disposition that predetermines our responses to situations and our interpretations of events. Mindset is a mental lens that shapes our everyday lives, guiding how we interpret experiences, setbacks, and opportunities. It can be thought of as the overarching narrative we carry with us, shaping our approach to life's challenges and successes. This mindset can be positive or negative and is typically shaped by many factors, including our upbringing, cultural background, and personal experiences. It can be categorized into different types, such as an innate growth mindset, an acquired growth mindset, or a growth mindset developed through effort and practice (Meier, n.d.; Pradeepa, 2022).

- **Attitudes** are our feelings or emotions toward particular subjects, objects, or events. They are often based on our underlying beliefs but can also be influenced by external factors like societal norms or experiences. Attitudes are reflected in how we feel about something and can be manifested in our behavior. They are less stable than beliefs and can change more readily in response to new information. Attitudes can be explicit, which are conscious and deliberate, or implicit, which are automatic and can influence our behavior without conscious awareness (Johnson, 2023; Pradeepa, 2022).
- **Beliefs** are the convictions we hold to be true, often without the requirement for proof. They are the fundamental truths we accept about ourselves, others, and the world. Beliefs can be explicit, which we can consciously articulate, or implicit, which are not consciously identified. They are usually deeply ingrained and can resist change, even when confronted with contrary evidence. Beliefs shape our behavior and decisions and are key to our identity and cultural belonging (Johnson, 2023).

Examples of Mindset

Mindsets shape how we view ourselves and the world around us, influencing our behaviors, decisions, and how we approach challenges and opportunities. Beyond the commonly discussed growth and fixed mindsets, several other mindsets play crucial roles in our lives. Here's a brief overview, including examples for clearer understanding:

- **Growth Mindset**: This mindset is characterized by the belief that abilities and intelligence can be developed with effort, practice, and persistence. Someone with a growth mindset might see a challenging task as an opportunity to grow and learn, even if they initially fail.
- **Fixed Mindset**: In contrast, a fixed mindset entails believing that abilities and intelligence are static and unchangeable. A person with a fixed mindset might avoid challenges, fearing failure will expose a lack of inherent ability.
- **Abundance Mindset**: Individuals with an abundance mindset believe there are enough resources and successes to share with others. They focus on the possibilities and opportunities, leading to optimism and generosity.
- **Scarcity Mindset**: Conversely, a scarcity mindset is dominated by the idea that there's a limited amount of resources or successes available, leading to competitiveness, jealousy, and negativity about others' achievements (*Mindset Matters*, n.d.).

- **Positive Mindset**: A positive mindset emphasizes looking on the bright side and expecting good things to happen. It's about focusing on strengths, seeking solutions, and feeling hopeful even in difficult times.
- **Negative Mindset**: This mindset dwells on the negative aspects of situations, expecting the worst and often experiencing a self-fulfilling prophecy of failure or disappointment. It can lead to a lack of motivation and feeling stuck in life's challenges (Logie, 2020).

Beyond these, there are several other mindsets worth noting:

- **Productive Mindset**: Believes in the value of hard work and productivity, focusing on accomplishing tasks and achieving goals efficiently.
- **Political Mindset**: Views success in terms of navigating social or organizational politics, emphasizing the importance of alliances, influence, and strategic interactions.
- **Win-Win Mindset**: Seeks solutions and agreements that benefit all parties involved, believing mutual benefit is the best outcome.
- **Win-Lose Mindset**: Believes that for one person to succeed, another must fail, viewing situations as zero-sum games.
- **Risk-Taking Mindset**: Willing to take calculated risks for potential rewards, seeing risk as an opportunity rather than something to avoid.

- **Control Mindset**: Desires to maintain strict control over situations and outcomes, often struggling with unpredictability and change (Spacey, 2020).

How Mindset Is Formed

By fostering environments that emphasize growth, resilience, and the value of effort over innate ability, we can cultivate mindsets conducive to learning, adaptation, and overall success (Cherry, 2022). Understanding the elements that shape our mindset reveals that it is a fluid characteristic that can be cultivated and strengthened through time.

Childhood Influences and Personal Experiences

From the moment we are born, our mindset begins to form. Children are inherently born with a love of learning, driven by curiosity and the necessity to explore their environment (Vermeer, 2012). However, how adults respond to and label children's abilities and efforts can stifle this natural inclination toward growth. When children are praised for their innate intelligence rather than their effort, it may encourage a fixed mindset, leading to a reluctance to engage in tasks that challenge their perceived capabilities (Vermeer, 2012). Furthermore, the labels and dialogues we are exposed to, such as being classified as the "smart one" or the "athletic one," can cement limiting beliefs that shape our self-perception and potential (Johnson, 2020).

Socialization and Environment

The environment, including our family, friends, and educational system, significantly impacts our mindset development. An environment that emphasizes growth, learning, and resilience fosters a growth mindset. This contrasts with environments that reward innate talent and discourage failure, potentially leading to a fixed mindset (Vermeer, 2012). Our surroundings, including the people we interact with and our physical space, can either bolster a positive mindset or contribute to a negative one, influencing our productivity and well-being (Durden, 2021).

Influence of Personality

Our personality traits, while inherent to some degree, also interact with our mindset. Some personalities may naturally gravitate toward a more positive or negative mindset, but it's crucial to recognize that our mindsets are malleable and can be influenced by conscious effort and reflection (Durden, 2021).

The Impact of Mindset

Mindset plays a pivotal role in shaping our success and achievements across various life domains, including academics, relationships, career, health and well-being, and personal development. Our beliefs, attitudes, and perspectives significantly influence how we perceive and respond to the world around us, guiding our actions, reactions, and overall approach to life's challenges and opportunities.

- **Academics:** In academics, the contrast between a growth mindset and a fixed mindset can greatly determine a student's performance and well-being. A study involving 600,000 15-year-olds across 78 countries found that students with a growth mindset performed significantly better academically than their peers with a fixed mindset. This mindset also correlated with greater well-being, illustrating the deep impact of believing in the potential for intelligence development through effort and perseverance (Sparks, 2021).
- **Relationships:** Mindset also plays a crucial role in relationships. Individuals with a growth mindset tend to seek partners who challenge them and help them grow, leading to more fulfilling and dynamic relationships. Conversely, those with a fixed mindset often look for validation of their perceived perfection, leading to stagnation and potential toxicity in relationships. Understanding and embracing the concept of growth and change within oneself and one's partner can lead to more meaningful connections (Adrian, 2020).
- **Career:** In career development, a positive and growth-oriented mindset encourages taking risks, seizing opportunities, and viewing setbacks as learning experiences rather than failures. This approach boosts confidence and fosters a willingness to learn and grow, significantly impacting one's career trajectory (Allemand, 2023; *How Does Mindset Impact Relationships?* n.d.).

- **Health and Well-Being:** Mindset influences health and well-being by affecting how individuals approach their health challenges and overall lifestyle choices. A positive mindset can lead to healthier behaviors, resilience in the face of illness or setbacks, and a more proactive attitude toward maintaining wellness (Graham, 2018).
- **Personal Development:** Finally, in personal development, a growth mindset is instrumental in overcoming challenges, learning from failures, and continuously striving for self-improvement. It empowers individuals to view every experience as an opportunity for growth, fostering motivation, resilience, and a lifelong commitment to learning and self-discovery (Agrawal, 2023; *How Does Mindset Impact Personal Growth?*).

Is Mindset Changeable?

If you're on the path to personal growth, know that changing your mindset isn't just a possibility—it's within your reach. Your brain is capable of remarkable transformations, no matter where you are in life's journey. Thanks to neuroscience, the concept of a fixed, unchangeable mindset is rapidly becoming outdated. Research into neuroplasticity and the impact of interventions on mindset has revolutionized our understanding of the brain's capability to change, grow, and adapt over time.

Neuroplasticity, a term that combines "neuro" (referring to neurons, the nerve cells that make up the brain) with "plasticity" (indicating malleability), describes the brain's incredible ability to continually reorganize itself by forming new neural connections throughout life. This ability is not limited by age, as once thought, but continues to offer potential for cognitive and emotional growth well into adulthood (Cherry, 2022b).

One compelling example of neuroplasticity in action is the work of Polish neuroscientist Jerzy Konorski, who coined the term in 1948. His and subsequent studies, particularly those by Michael Merzenich, dubbed the "father of neuroplasticity," have shown that the brain retains its ability to learn and grow throughout our entire lives through experiences, learning, and environmental factors, debunking the myth that our mental capacities are fixed post-childhood (*How to Change Your Mindset*, 2022).

Furthermore, the distinction between "fixed" and "growth" mindsets, which we have already begun to explore, adds another layer to our understanding. We have some agency here. Those with a fixed mindset view their abilities as static, hindering their capacity to learn from challenges and failures. In contrast, individuals with a growth mindset see challenges as opportunities for development, believing that effort and perseverance can lead to mastery and intelligence (Primeau, 2021). We can consciously shift from one of these mindsets to another.

Changing your mindset is possible and instrumental in fostering personal development and overcoming obstacles. Adopting a positive mindset can significantly alter life's trajectory, encouraging resilience, optimism, and a willingness to embrace change and challenges (Newlyn, 2022).

Transformative Journeys

Our lives are often defined by our circumstances and how we perceive and react to them. These stories from Sofia, Emma, and Lucas illustrate how deliberate changes in mindset can lead to profound transformations in personal happiness, confidence, and professional success.

Sofia's Shift to Positivity

Sofia constantly focused on the negatives in her life, which affected her happiness and relationships. She realized she needed to shift her mindset to a more positive outlook to change her life's trajectory. Sofia's specific goal was "I want to focus on the positives in my life to improve my overall happiness and strengthen my relationships."

She identified the behaviors and mindset changes required: consciously identifying positive aspects of her day, practicing gratitude, and replacing negative thoughts with positive affirmations. Each morning, Sofia reviewed her goal and prepared herself to recognize and celebrate the positives. Whenever she caught herself dwelling on the negative, she would redirect her thoughts with affirmations like "I choose to see the good in this situation" and "I am surrounded by abundance."

This process required deliberate effort, especially in challenging situations. However, as Sofia consistently practiced her affirmations and sought the positives, her outlook changed. Positivity became her new default, greatly enhancing her quality of life and relationships. Through intentional effort and practice, Sofia transformed her internal monologue and, with it, her life.

Emma's Journey to Confidence

Emma always struggled with self-confidence, particularly when it came to public speaking. She dreaded presentations and would avoid situations where she had to speak in front of others. Realizing that her fear was holding her back professionally, Emma changed her mindset. She began by writing down her goal: "I want to be confident in public speaking because it will open more professional opportunities and help me share my ideas effectively."

She then outlined the mindset and behavior changes needed: practicing public speaking in smaller, less intimidating settings, joining a local Toastmasters club to get structured feedback, and affirming her worth and ability to communicate effectively every day. Each morning, Emma reviewed her goals and the changes she was striving to make. She repeated affirmations like "I am a confident and effective communicator" and "My ideas are worth sharing."

Initially, these actions required significant effort, but they became more natural over time. Emma started to volunteer for speaking opportunities, and with each success, her confidence grew. She no longer needed to consciously remind herself of her affirmations; they had become ingrained in her thought process. Emma's deliberate effort to change her mindset transformed her into a confident speaker, admired by her colleagues for her eloquence and clarity.

Lucas's Path to a Growth Mindset

Lucas was a talented software developer but often avoided challenging projects, fearing failure. He believed that talent was fixed, and if he struggled, it meant he wasn't good enough. After missing out on several exciting opportunities, Lucas decided it was time for a change. He wrote down his goal: "I want to embrace challenging projects to grow my skills and advance my career."

Lucas identified the need to adopt a growth mindset. He committed to viewing challenges as opportunities for learning and growth rather than threats to his competence. Each morning, he reminded himself, "Effort and learning lead to growth," and "Challenges help me become a better developer."

It wasn't easy at first, and Lucas had to consciously choose to tackle difficult tasks he would have previously avoided. He also started verbalizing his new beliefs, saying, "I can learn and improve" whenever he encountered setbacks. Over time, these decisions and affirmations reshaped his mindset. Lucas became known for his willingness to take on the most challenging projects, and his career flourished.

Summary

- **Contrasting Reactions to Setbacks**: The story of Alex and Jamie illustrates the stark difference between a fixed and a growth mindset. While Alex sees rejection as a confirmation of inadequacy (fixed mindset), Jamie views it as an opportunity for growth and learning (growth mindset), setting the stage for their future paths and successes.
- **Definition and Impact of Mindset**: Mindset, the set of beliefs about ourselves and our capabilities, profoundly influences our behavior, decision-making, and how we face challenges. Adopting a growth mindset, which views talents and abilities as qualities that can be developed, positively impacts various life aspects, including academic achievement, relationships, career progression, health, and personal growth.
- **Formation of Mindset**: Factors such as childhood experiences, socialization, environment, and inherent personality traits play crucial roles in shaping our mindset. For example, early praise for effort rather than innate intelligence can foster a growth mindset conducive to lifelong learning and resilience.
- **Changeability of Mindset**: Insights from neuroplasticity underscore that mindsets are not static but can be shifted from fixed to growth through conscious effort and practice. This adaptability suggests that personal development and overcoming challenges are achievable by altering our mindset.

- **Transformative Journeys**: Real-life examples of individuals like Emma, Lucas, and Sofia, who successfully changed their mindsets, demonstrate the practical steps and outcomes of embracing growth, positivity, and challenge. These stories highlight the profound personal and professional benefits of mindset transformation.

Conclusion

As we finish this chapter, we've explored how our mindset—how we think and feel about our abilities—touches every part of our lives. The story of Alex and Jamie showed us that the way we react to things like job rejections matters. Jamie's positive and open mindset teaches us an important lesson: Our mindset shapes our life, turning obstacles into opportunities for growth. Then, Sofia, Emma, and Lucas showcased the transformative power of a mindset shift, proving that with intentional effort and a change in perspective, we can overcome personal barriers and achieve our fullest potential.

Next, we're going to look at limiting beliefs. These hidden thoughts hold us back, even though we might not always see them. They're powerful and can stop us from reaching our full potential. We'll learn how these beliefs are formed, how they affect us, and, most importantly, how we can challenge and change them. By figuring out how to fight against negative thoughts, we start breaking free from the limits we unknowingly placed on ourselves.

Part 2
Patterns Holding You Back from Progress

Chapter 2
Breaking the Chains of Limiting Beliefs

At the dawn of the 20th century, Madam C.J. Walker faced a world that seemed stacked against her. Born to recently freed slaves, she encountered the harsh realities of post-Civil War America—a society marked by deep racial and gender prejudices. Her early years were fraught with challenges, including a labor-intensive childhood, a troubled marriage, and severe hair loss stemming from poor health and stress. This last issue, though seemingly minor, symbolized the larger struggles in her life—obstacles that seemed insurmountable due to her race and sex.

However, Madam Walker's story didn't end there. Motivated by her own needs and the widespread lack of hair care products for African American women, she began experimenting with remedies at home. Despite numerous setbacks and widespread skepticism—even from her own community—who doubted the feasibility of a Black woman creating a successful business, Walker refused to let these limiting beliefs define her capabilities.

Her journey from a laundress earning barely a dollar a day to the first female self-made millionaire in America is a testament to her genius and a striking example of overcoming limiting beliefs. Beyond promising beauty, each bottle of her hair care product spoke of a barrier broken, a silent protest against the societal limits imposed on Black women.

As we explore the significance of self-talk in the upcoming discussion, remember Madam Walker. Her story is poised to inspire us to question and transform our internal dialogues. How did she silence the doubts within and the discouragement from others? Stay tuned as we explore how the words we tell ourselves can either confine or liberate us, much like they did for Madam C.J. Walker.

What Are Limiting Beliefs?

Limiting beliefs are invisible barriers we place around ourselves based on the assumption that we can't achieve or don't deserve success in various aspects of our lives. Imagine telling yourself, "I'm not good at public speaking," so you avoid opportunities to present your ideas, even though it could lead to professional advancement. These beliefs are not just about doubting our abilities—they also include ideas about how the world works or what we deserve from life, which can significantly hold us back from pursuing our goals and dreams (Wooll, 2022).

The roots of limiting beliefs are diverse, often stemming from early life experiences, societal norms, cultural values, and personal encounters. From childhood, we're influenced by our family's beliefs and values, absorbing them even before we're fully aware. These foundational beliefs shape our view of ourselves and the world. For instance, if a family emphasizes that success is unattainable without extreme sacrifice, we might avoid pursuing ambitious goals for fear of losing something valuable in our lives (Wooll, 2022).

Similarly, our social environment, including interactions with peers and educators, plays a crucial role in developing these beliefs. Negative experiences, such as bullying or criticism from authority figures, can implant a belief in our inadequacy or unworthiness. This effect is not limited to direct interactions; observed behaviors and expressed attitudes within our community can also lead us to internalize limiting beliefs about what is possible or appropriate for us (Matthews, 2020).

Moreover, the impact of these beliefs extends beyond personal development. In the workplace, they can stifle creativity, reduce morale, and hinder the pursuit of innovative solutions. When we doubt our capabilities or potential, we're less likely to propose new ideas or take on challenges, leading to a culture of stagnation rather than growth (*10 Limiting Beliefs*, 2021).

Overcoming these limiting beliefs requires conscious effort and strategies. Identifying and challenging these beliefs is the first step, followed by actively seeking experiences that contradict them. For example, engaging in positive affirmations, seeking feedback, and pushing ourselves to step outside our comfort zones can help shift our mindset from one of limitation to one of possibility (Wooll, 2022).

Overcoming limiting beliefs leads to a significant inner transformation. By challenging and changing these beliefs, we begin to see ourselves and our potential in a new light. This process requires a commitment to self-awareness, positive self-talk, and the courage to step out of our comfort zones. As we embrace this inner change, we unlock our true capabilities and pave the way for personal growth and fulfillment. Ultimately, understanding that limiting beliefs are not inherent truths but perspectives shaped by our experiences and environment empowers us to break free from them, driving the transformation that leads to realizing our full potential.

Examples of Limiting Beliefs

These limiting beliefs are just narratives we tell ourselves, and recognizing them is the first step toward challenging and eventually overcoming them.

- **I am unworthy of love.** This belief can severely impact your relationships and self-esteem, making you feel undeserving of affection and kindness from others.
- **I cannot trust anyone in my life.** This belief fosters isolation and hinders the development of meaningful connections with others.
- **I am a horrible person.** Such a belief can lead to a negative self-image and prevent you from seeing your true value and potential.

- **I'm not good enough.** This common limiting belief can affect various areas of your life, making you feel inadequate no matter your achievements.
- **I'm too old.** This belief can stop you from pursuing new opportunities or learning new skills based on the assumption that it's too late to start something new
- **I'm too young.** Conversely, this belief may lead you to think you lack the experience or credibility to achieve your goals, which can halt progress and growth.
- **I'm not smart enough.** This can affect your confidence in your intellectual abilities, limiting your educational or career advancements.
- **I don't deserve happiness.** Believing this can prevent you from seeking out or accepting opportunities that could lead to joy and fulfillment.
- **Everything is my fault.** If you believe you're always to blame, you may take on unnecessary guilt, hindering your ability to move forward positively.
- **I don't have the correct experience.** This belief might stop you from applying for jobs or positions where you could otherwise excel with the skills you do have.
- **I shouldn't speak up because being quiet and agreeable is better.** Holding onto this belief can prevent you from expressing your thoughts and contributing valuable ideas.
- **I am too broken for a relationship.** Such a belief undermines your self-worth and can keep you from engaging in healthy, fulfilling relationships.

- **I grew up poor, so I will always be poor.** This belief limits your financial growth and mindset, suggesting that your past will always define your financial future.
- **I can't change my situation.** Feeling trapped by this belief can lead to passivity and prevent you from taking steps toward change.
- **My colleagues are far more knowledgeable on this subject.** Thinking this way can deter you from contributing your ideas and growing professionally (Kristenson, 2023; Tanasugarn, 2022).

The Impact of Limiting Beliefs

Limiting beliefs are often deeply ingrained assumptions that constrain our lives in many ways, subtly dictating our decisions and shaping our future. These beliefs, stemming from past experiences, societal messages, or self-imposed standards, can significantly impede our ability to achieve our fullest potential. Whether it's a missed job opportunity due to self-doubt, reluctance in pursuing relationships because of fear of rejection, or a lack of personal growth due to a fear of failure, these invisible barriers can have profound effects (Kachigan, 2021; Van Horn, 2023):

- **Mental Health and Happiness:** Limiting beliefs act as barriers to personal growth and fulfillment. For instance, someone may avoid applying for their dream job, fearing they aren't skilled enough to get it, or they may not pursue a passion because they were told they wouldn't be successful. This can lead to feelings of

inadequacy, low self-esteem, and even depression as individuals internalize these beliefs as truths about their capabilities.
- **Relationships:** In intimate relationships, limiting beliefs such as fear of vulnerability or doubts about self-worth can prevent deep and meaningful connections. Past experiences, such as witnessing failed relationships or internalizing negative comments from childhood, can lead individuals to avoid intimacy, mistrust others, or stay in unhealthy relationships, thinking they do not deserve better.
- **Performance:** At work, limiting beliefs can manifest as self-doubt, reduced confidence, and a lack of motivation, which can impede professional growth. Individuals may not seek promotions, hesitate to contribute ideas, or avoid challenging tasks, fearing failure or rejection. This affects their career trajectory and can contribute to a toxic work environment by stifling creativity and collaboration.
- **Staying in the Comfort Zone:** Limiting beliefs keeps individuals in their comfort zones, where they avoid risks and new experiences, thereby stifling creativity and growth. For example, someone might have a limiting belief that they are not creative or innovative, leading them to shy away from opportunities that require out-of-the-box thinking. This resistance to stepping out of one's comfort zone can lead to missed opportunities for personal and professional development.

- **Hindering Growth and Creativity:** Creativity and personal growth are essential for a fulfilling life, yet limiting beliefs can severely restrict these aspects. A person who believes they are not creative enough or too old to learn new skills will likely not pursue hobbies or interests that could enhance their quality of life and bring them joy. As a result, they miss out on discovering new passions or developing talents that could enrich their lives and the lives of those around them.
- **Sabotaging Success:** The fear of failure is a common limiting belief that can sabotage success. Individuals may not set ambitious goals or take on challenging projects due to a fear of not succeeding, leading to a self-fulfilling prophecy where the lack of action ensures failure. This cycle of fear and inaction can prevent individuals from reaching their full potential and experiencing the satisfaction of achieving their goals.

Identifying Your Limiting Beliefs

Recognizing that we create our own lives through our beliefs and actions is empowering. Our mindset and internal narratives greatly influence our decisions and paths. By identifying and challenging limiting beliefs, we open ourselves to new possibilities and growth opportunities. This proactive approach enables us to take control of our lives and shape them according to our true potential.

Limiting beliefs act as invisible barriers to our growth and fulfillment. These beliefs are often ingrained in us early on through family values, educational experiences, and personal encounters, shaping how we view ourselves and our potential in the world. Whether it's a belief that we're not good enough, too old, or unworthy of love, these narratives can significantly hold us back.

Recognizing your own limiting beliefs is crucial for personal development. One effective way to do this is by paying close attention to recurring thoughts and patterns that may be self-defeating. These often manifest as internal narratives criticizing or doubting your abilities and worth. Writing these thoughts down creates a tangible record that can be analyzed and questioned. This process can help you identify areas where you feel stuck or unfulfilled, shedding light on the underlying beliefs that may hold you back (Matthews, 2020).

To facilitate this recognition, engage in reflective practices such as journaling. Write about situations where you felt limited or unable to pursue your goals and ask yourself why. Consider the origins of these beliefs—were they taught to you by family members, influenced by past experiences, or adopted from societal norms? Reflecting on these questions can help you pinpoint the root causes of your limiting beliefs, making them easier to address and overcome (Wooll, 2022b).

Once identified, challenging and replacing these limiting beliefs with empowering ones is key. This involves questioning their validity and consciously adopting new, more positive beliefs that align with your goals and aspirations. It's a process that requires commitment and may benefit from the support of counseling or coaching, where professionals can offer strategies and insights to facilitate change.

Consider using the blank pages at the end of the book for journaling as you explore these additional questions designed to help you reveal your limiting beliefs (Pasha, 2017; Van Horn, 2023; Yugay, 2022):

- What areas of your life do you feel most stuck or unsatisfied with, and why do you think that is?
- Can you identify any recurring negative thoughts about yourself or your abilities? How do these thoughts affect your actions or decisions?
- Reflect on your childhood and upbringing. Are there any beliefs or values you've inherited from your family that might be holding you back?
- Think about a goal you've struggled to achieve. What beliefs about yourself or the situation do you think are preventing you from reaching this goal?
- Have you ever avoided pursuing an opportunity because you feared failure, rejection, or judgment? What was the belief underlying that fear?
- Are there any areas where you often blame external circumstances or others for your lack of progress? What does this suggest about your beliefs regarding control and responsibility in your life?
- Consider the last time you were really proud of something you accomplished. What positive beliefs about yourself were confirmed by this achievement?

- Have you ever been surprised by achieving something you didn't think was possible? What limiting belief did this experience challenge?
- In what situations do you feel envious or resentful of others' successes? What do these feelings reveal about your own beliefs regarding success and worthiness?
- Imagine a life without your current limiting beliefs. How would your actions, relationships, and goals change?

Changing Self-Talk

The role of self-talk in reinforcing limiting beliefs and perpetuating negative thought patterns is significant because it shapes how we perceive ourselves and our capabilities. Self-talk is our internal dialogue, reflecting our thoughts, beliefs, and biases. This inner voice can be supportive and positive or negative and undermining. Negative self-talk focuses on our perceived shortcomings and failures, reinforcing limiting beliefs by convincing us of our inability to achieve goals or change negative patterns.

Transforming limiting beliefs starts with addressing your internal monologue. The way you talk to yourself shapes your self-perception and capabilities. Shifting from negative self-talk to positive affirmations helps create a supportive mindset. This change is not about ignoring challenges but about approaching them with confidence in your ability to overcome and learn from them.

For example, if someone repeatedly tells themselves, "I'm not good enough to pursue this career," they're likely to avoid taking steps toward such goals, further entrenching the belief that they are incapable. This negative self-talk can become a self-fulfilling prophecy, where the individual's actions (or lack thereof) confirm their limiting beliefs, creating a cycle that's hard to break. Negative self-talk often exaggerates the truth, leading to rumination and focusing on negative outcomes without considering positive possibilities or past successes (*Self-Talk*, 2022).

Cultivating positive self-talk is crucial to counteract limiting beliefs and build self-confidence and resilience. Positive self-talk involves consciously shifting your internal dialogue to be more supportive, encouraging, and kind to yourself. It means recognizing when you're engaging in negative self-talk and intentionally replacing those thoughts with positive affirmations or more balanced perspectives. This practice can help reduce stress, improve mental health, and lead to better outcomes in various areas of life, from personal relationships to professional achievements.

Positive self-talk encourages a growth mindset, where challenges are seen as opportunities for learning and growth rather than insurmountable obstacles. By focusing on strengths, achievements, and potential, positive self-talk can help dismantle limiting beliefs, enabling individuals to approach their goals with confidence and resilience. It's a key component in developing a healthier self-image and a more optimistic outlook on life, which are essential for personal growth and happiness.

To cultivate positive self-talk, one can start by becoming aware of negative thought patterns and challenging them with evidence from their own experiences that contradict these limiting beliefs (Legg, 2016). Setting realistic, achievable goals and celebrating small successes can also reinforce the benefits of positive self-talk. Over time, this practice can significantly impact one's belief in one's abilities, opening up new possibilities for achievement and fulfillment.

Recalling the journey of Madam C.J. Walker, we see a powerful example of overcoming negative self-talk. Faced with the societal belief that a Black woman could neither own a successful business nor revolutionize beauty standards, Walker could have succumbed to the chorus of doubts and discouragements. However, she chose to challenge this narrative. Instead of internalizing the skepticism and limitations placed upon her, she rephrased her self-talk from "I can't be a successful businesswoman because of my race and gender" to "I am capable of success regardless of the barriers in front of me." This shift in mindset changed her self-perception and propelled her to take bold actions that defied the restrictive norms of her time. Her success story illustrates how transforming our internal dialogue can lead to extraordinary achievements and break through limiting beliefs.

Positive Affirmations

Positive affirmations are short, affirming statements that, when repeated frequently, can help to shift your focus from negative or limiting beliefs to a more positive and supportive perspective. This practice is grounded in the principle of neuroplasticity, which suggests that the brain can form new connections and pathways based on our thoughts and experiences (Goldman, 2022). By consciously choosing to affirm positive thoughts about ourselves, we can begin to dismantle the old patterns of negative self-talk and build new, more positive ones.

- **Choose your affirmations.** Begin by selecting affirmations that resonate with you and address areas where you seek improvement or support. These might relate to self-confidence, resilience, health, or any other aspect of your life where you wish to foster positive change.
- **Repeat them regularly.** To be effective, affirmations must be repeated frequently and with conviction. Consider setting aside specific times of the day, such as in the morning or before bed, to focus on your affirmations. Repetition is key to embedding these positive messages into your subconscious.
- **Incorporate them into your daily life.** Beyond dedicated repetition times, look for opportunities to remind yourself of your affirmations throughout the day. This could be through notes placed in visible locations, setting reminders on your phone, or even incorporating them into your journaling practice.
- **Feel the affirmations.** It's important not just to say the affirmations but to truly feel them. Try to evoke the emotions and sensations you associate with the truth of each affirmation as you repeat it. This emotional engagement can help to reinforce the positive message within your subconscious.

- **Be patient and persistent.** Like any form of mental training, cultivating positive self-talk through affirmations takes time and consistency. Be patient with yourself and persistent in your practice. Over time, you'll notice shifts in your mindset and attitudes.

Examples of Positive Affirmations

- I am capable of achieving my goals.
- I am worthy of love and respect.
- I am resilient and can overcome challenges.
- I am a positive force in the world.
- I believe in my ability to succeed.
- I am grateful for the abundance in my life.
- I trust the journey of my life.
- I choose happiness and positivity.
- I am deserving of my dreams.
- I am strong and confident.
- I radiate peace and kindness.
- I am in control of my happiness.
- I embrace my unique talents and qualities.
- I am a constant learner and grow every day.
- I am surrounded by love and positivity.

Crafting Your Affirmations: A Guide

Affirmations work best when they're personal. Use the blank pages at the end of this book to write them down. Here's how to create ones that fit your journey (Picardi, 2022):

1. **Start with "I am."** Affirmations are most effective when they begin with "I am," anchoring the statement in the present and making it inherently personal. For instance, "I am capable of achieving my dreams."
2. **Stay present.** Write your affirmations in the present tense to affirm that the change you seek is currently happening. This helps in creating a mindset that your goals are within reach.
3. **Be specific.** Focus on specific areas you wish to transform or enhance. Whether it's confidence, peace, success, or health, tailor your affirmations to address these directly.
4. **Embrace positivity.** Frame your affirmations positively, focusing on what you want to attract rather than what you wish to avoid.
5. **Keep it real.** Ensure your affirmations are believable and achievable. They should stretch and challenge you but remain grounded in your reality.

Summary

- **Definition and Nature of Limiting Beliefs:** Limiting beliefs are unconscious assumptions that hold us back from achieving our potential. These beliefs, often formed by past experiences and societal influences, affect our self-esteem, decisions, and behaviors.
- **Examples and Identification:** Common limiting beliefs include fears of inadequacy and unworthiness. Identifying these requires introspection and

understanding their roots in past experiences or societal teachings.
- **Impact of Limiting Beliefs:** They affect our mental health, relationships, work performance, and personal growth by keeping us in our comfort zones, hindering creativity, and promoting fear of failure.
- **Overcoming Limiting Beliefs:** This involves changing negative self-talk to positive and using affirmations based on the brain's ability to rewire itself (neuroplasticity). This shift can break down negative beliefs and support growth.
- **Crafting Personal Affirmations:** Effective affirmations are specific, positive, and in the present tense. They require regular repetition, patience, and emotional engagement to change mindsets. Personalizing these affirmations to individual needs is crucial.

Conclusion

In this chapter, we explored how limiting beliefs can hold us back from reaching our full potential. We saw how these beliefs form from past experiences and societal messages, telling us we're not good enough or don't deserve success. But we also learned that we can challenge these beliefs. By recognizing and questioning them and using positive self-talk and affirmations, we can break free from these invisible barriers.

Next, we'll dive into common negative thinking patterns that keep us in a cycle of self-defeating behavior. We'll introduce techniques like cognitive restructuring and thought records, which help us change these negative thoughts. This next step is crucial for continuing our journey toward personal growth and breaking free from the chains of negative thinking.

Chapter 3
Breaking the Cycle of Negative Thinking

Can you imagine navigating through an afternoon filled with over 6,000 thoughts? You do it every day. This astounding figure isn't just a random guess—it's rooted in scientific research. A study, widely discussed and confirmed by researchers at Queen's University, unveiled that the average person transitions through more than 6,000 thoughts daily (Raypole, 2022). These "thought worms," as the researchers termed them, represent moments when our brain hops from one topic to another, revealing the incredible complexity and dynamism of our internal lives.

Yet, amidst this constant stream of thoughts, a significant number lean toward the negative. These negative thoughts can profoundly influence our emotions, behaviors, and overall well-being. Negative thinking patterns can ensnare us, shaping our perceptions and interactions with the world in a way that reinforces pessimism and despair. It's a cycle that can be tough to break, given the natural human tendency to give more weight to negative experiences—a phenomenon known as the negativity bias.

Recognizing the patterns of our thoughts and the power they wield over our lives is the first step toward change. By reflecting on the quality of our thoughts and their impact on our daily experiences, we can identify the negative patterns that hold us back. This awareness is crucial for anyone looking to break free from the cycle of negative thinking and foster a more positive, resilient mindset.

Cognitive restructuring techniques offer a path forward. These strategies (which will be explained in more detail) challenge us to confront and reframe our negative thoughts, transforming them into more balanced and constructive ones. Additionally, thought records serve as a practical tool in this endeavor, allowing us to document and analyze our thoughts to identify patterns and triggers of negativity.

By applying these techniques, we can gradually shift our internal dialogue from one that is self-defeating to one that is empowering. The journey isn't always easy, but the rewards—increased emotional well-being, enhanced resilience, and a more fulfilling life—are worth the effort. Let this chapter serve as a guide to recognizing, challenging, and changing the negative thought patterns that limit us, paving the way for a brighter, more positive future.

What Are Negative Thinking Patterns?

Negative thinking patterns, called cognitive distortions, embody recurrent and unrealistic negative thoughts regarding oneself and one's environment. It's part of the human condition to occasionally grapple with negative thoughts. However, when negativity pervades to the point of significantly altering one's self-perception and worldview, impairing everyday functionality, it becomes a profound concern for mental well-being and life quality. Such patterns have the potential to trigger or intensify mental health issues, including depression, anxiety disorders, personality disorders, and schizophrenia (Smith, 2022).

Various factors contribute to the emergence of negative thinking. These can range from experiences that cause trauma or distress, such as bullying, academic challenges, or the death of a loved one, to social pressures and an absence of effective coping mechanisms. Conditions like anxiety and depression, perfectionism stemming from unattainably high standards, and other health issues that adversely affect self-esteem are also significant contributors. Moreover, mental health conditions, including Obsessive-Compulsive Disorder (OCD), Generalized Anxiety Disorder (GAD), and depression, are known to aggravate the cycle of negative thinking patterns.

Strategies to counter negative thinking include cognitive restructuring, which helps individuals identify and transform negative thoughts into positive ones; mindfulness, enhancing awareness of thoughts as they occur; positive self-talk, encouraging a kinder and more constructive inner dialogue; visualization and reframing, imagining oneself in positive scenarios; journaling to identify and track negative thoughts; and seeking social support to counter feelings of isolation and enhance self-confidence (Vallejo, 2023).

The Impact of Negative Thinking

Negative thinking patterns can perpetuate a cycle of negativity, leading to feelings of hopelessness and despair, and contribute to stress, anxiety, or low self-esteem. This cycle can profoundly impact various areas of life, including relationships, work, and overall well-being. In a world where so little is under our control, the one thing we can govern is ourselves—our thoughts, reactions, and attitudes. Recognizing this power is transformative. By focusing on what we can control, we reclaim our ability to shape our mental landscape. This awareness is crucial as it sets the stage for using cognitive restructuring and thought records to guide us toward a more positive and resilient mindset.

Relationships: Negative thinking patterns often lead to doubt about one's abilities and reinforce negative beliefs about oneself, making it challenging to engage fully in social situations. This can lead to withdrawal from social interactions, damaging meaningful relationships with family, friends, and romantic partners. Negative thinking can cause individuals to blame others, overdramatize situations, and avoid confronting relationship issues, ultimately leading to self-loathing and avoiding new meaningful connections (*How Does Negative Thinking Affect Your Social Skills?* 2022).

Work: In the workplace, negative thinking can manifest as a lack of confidence and fear of engagement, impacting communication with colleagues and productivity. Individuals may experience stress over minor tasks due to catastrophic thinking, fearing the worst outcomes, and doubting their abilities, which can diminish their performance and career progression (*Negative Thought Patterns and Depression*, 2022).

Overall Well-being: On a broader scale, negative thinking can significantly affect mental health, leading to depression, anxiety, and panic attacks. It reinforces feelings of worthlessness and can cause individuals to engage in self-destructive behaviors, such as substance abuse, as a form of coping with the dissatisfaction and disappointment in their lives. This ongoing cycle of negativity can also lead to physical health issues, such as chronic stress, which has been linked to a host of physical health problems (Digit Insurance, 2023).

Moreover, negative thinking is associated with rapid mood shifts and reduced self-esteem and energy levels, making it difficult for individuals to maintain a positive outlook on life. This can further exacerbate conditions such as Obsessive-Compulsive Disorder (OCD) and lead to the development of addiction as individuals seek ways to escape their negative thought patterns (*Effect of Negative Thinking*, n.d.).

After detailing the profound impacts of negative thinking on our relationships, work, and overall well-being, it becomes clear that the cycle of negativity is not just a personal issue but a pervasive one that affects many aspects of our lives. However, it's crucial to recognize that in this vast and often unpredictable world, the one domain we truly have control over is ourselves—our thoughts, our reactions, and our attitudes. Acknowledging this power is not just comforting; it's transformative. It sets the stage for introducing cognitive restructuring and thought records as practical tools for reclaiming that power, guiding us toward a more positive and resilient mindset.

Limiting Beliefs vs. Cognitive Distortions

To deepen your understanding of how your thought patterns influence your well-being, it's important to examine the relationship between limiting beliefs and cognitive distortions. Limiting beliefs are a specific category of cognitive distortions that focus on your abilities, worth, and potential. These negative thoughts suggest you are confined in some significant way, often manifesting as deep-seated convictions about your incapacity to achieve success, happiness, or fulfillment in different areas of your life. For instance, you might believe that you are fundamentally unlovable or that professional success is unattainable.

While all limiting beliefs are cognitive distortions, not every cognitive distortion is a limiting belief. Cognitive distortions encompass a broader spectrum of irrational thought patterns, including black-and-white thinking, overgeneralization, and catastrophizing. These can distort any aspect of your reality, not just self-perceptions. For example, catastrophizing about a future event doesn't necessarily denote a limiting belief about your abilities, yet it represents an unhelpful and skewed thought pattern that can lead to undue stress and anxiety.

Common Negative Thinking Patterns

By recognizing these patterns and challenging their validity, you can start to break free from the cycle of negative thinking and move toward a more balanced and realistic view of yourself and your experiences (Casabianca, 2021; Garey, n.d.).

All-or-Nothing Thinking

- **Definition:** All-or-nothing thinking involves viewing situations in only two categories rather than on a spectrum. If something is not perfect, it is seen as a total failure.
- **Example:** Jane decides to eat healthier and successfully follows a nutritious diet for a week. However, one evening, she has a slice of cake at a party and then tells herself, "I've ruined my diet completely. I might as well give up." This thinking pattern fails to recognize her progress and disregards the concept of balance.

Disqualifying the Positive

- **Definition:** This pattern involves rejecting positive experiences or accomplishments, insisting they "don't count" for various reasons, thus maintaining a negative belief despite evidence to the contrary.
- **Example:** After receiving compliments on his presentation at work, Tom thinks, "They're just being nice. Anyone could have done that presentation." He

overlooks his effort and skill, focusing only on negatives.

Emotional Reasoning

- **Definition:** Emotional reasoning means assuming that negative emotions reflect the way things really are: "I feel it. Therefore, it must be true."
- **Example:** Lisa feels overwhelmed and thinks, "I feel like a bad mother, so it must be true," despite her dedication and love for her children, disqualifying her positive parenting moments.

Jumping to Conclusions

- **Definition:** This pattern involves making a negative interpretation without evidence. It includes mind reading (assuming the thoughts and intentions of others) and fortune telling (predicting things will turn out badly).
- **Example:** Kevin doesn't receive an immediate reply to his email and concludes, "My boss must be upset with me," without considering other reasons for the delay.

Mind Reading

- **Definition:** Mind reading occurs when someone assumes they know what others are thinking about them, usually in a negative way, without any concrete evidence.

- **Example:** Sarah sees her friends whispering and immediately thinks, "They must be talking about me. They don't like me," even though her friends were planning a surprise for her.

Fortune Telling

- **Definition:** Fortune telling is predicting that things will turn out badly without any evidence.
- **Example:** Before starting his new job, Alex thinks, "I'm going to be terrible at this and probably get fired," preemptively assuming failure.

Labeling and Mislabeling

- **Definition:** This involves attaching a negative label to oneself or others based on one instance or action, which is an extreme form of overgeneralization.
- **Example:** After forgetting her anniversary, Emily thinks, "I'm a terrible spouse," ignoring all her caring actions and contributions to the relationship.

Magnification (Catastrophizing) or Minimization

- **Definition:** Exaggerating the importance of negative details (magnification) or minimizing positive ones (minimization), skewing the perception of reality.
- **Example:** Jack makes a minor mistake at work and thinks, "This will ruin the entire project," magnifying the error's impact far beyond its actual significance.

Mental Filter

- **Definition:** Focusing exclusively on a negative detail and dwelling on it, which darkens the perception of a situation.
- **Example:** Despite receiving numerous compliments on her performance, Anita fixates on a single, mildly constructive criticism, allowing it to overshadow all positive feedback.

Overgeneralization

- **Definition:** Viewing a single negative event as a never-ending pattern of defeat by using absolute words like "always" or "never."
- **Example:** After a date cancels on him, Ben thinks, "I'll always be alone. No one ever wants to date me," despite it being a one-time occurrence.

Personalization

- **Definition:** Believing oneself to be the cause of external events or situations for which one is not primarily responsible.
- **Example:** When her son struggles in school, Marie blames herself entirely, saying, "If I were a better parent, he'd be doing better," disregarding other factors like the teaching methods or the son's individual challenges.

Should Statements

- **Definition:** Using "should" statements for motivation leads to feelings of guilt and failure when those expectations are not met.
- **Example:** Greg tells himself, "I should never feel angry at my kids," which makes him feel guilty when inevitable frustration arises, ignoring that feeling a range of emotions is human.

Cognitive Restructuring

Cognitive restructuring is a skill that improves with regular practice. It can be used both as a response to specific negative thoughts and as a daily ritual to cultivate a more positive mindset. Each time you engage in this process, you chip away at the power negative thinking has over your life, making room for more constructive and encouraging thoughts.

Embracing the power to release thoughts and patterns that no longer serve us is a way of clearing the clutter in our minds. Just as decluttering our living spaces can bring clarity and a sense of peace, so too can letting go of negative thought patterns and beliefs that hold us back. This act of release isn't just about getting rid of something; it's about making room for new, more empowering beliefs and experiences. It's a conscious choice to prioritize our mental health and well-being, recognizing that we deserve to live a life marked by resilience, positivity, and growth.

Cognitive restructuring involves recognizing negative thoughts and beliefs, scrutinizing them to assess their validity, and substituting them with thoughts or beliefs that are either more realistic or supportive. Let's break down this transformative process (Stanborough, 2020).

Identify Negative Thoughts

Begin by observing moments when you feel down, anxious, or upset. What thoughts are running through your mind at these times? Often, they are negative assumptions or forecasts, like fearing you'll fail an upcoming presentation or believing no one appreciates your efforts. Recognizing these thoughts is the first step toward cognitive restructuring.

Challenge These Thoughts

Next, question the basis of your negative thoughts. Are they rooted in facts or merely feelings? Could there be another explanation for the situation? If you're worried because a friend hasn't called back, consider that they might be tied up with something else rather than assuming they're ignoring you.

Replace These Thoughts

Develop a more balanced thought to take the place of the negative one. Instead of telling yourself you're bound to fail a presentation, remind yourself that you're well-prepared and it's okay to make mistakes. This step is about replacing destructive thoughts with ones more grounded in reality and kindness toward yourself.

By dedicating yourself to cognitive restructuring, you embark on self-discovery and empowerment. You learn to see challenges as opportunities for growth and to view yourself and the world around you more positively. This journey may not be easy, and old patterns of thought may persist, but with perseverance and patience, significant changes in your mental landscape are possible. If you find yourself struggling, consider seeking support from a cognitive behavioral therapist, who can guide you through the process with tailored strategies and insights.

When you start practicing cognitive restructuring, you're taking steps to understand yourself better and become stronger. You'll begin to see hard times as chances to grow and to think more positively about yourself and everything around you. This process can be tough, and old ways of thinking might not go away quickly, but if you keep at it, you can change how you think (Zorbas, 2023).

Thought Records

A thought record is a key technique in Cognitive Behavioral Therapy (CBT) that helps you track and challenge negative thoughts. It involves reflecting on a specific situation that triggered negative feelings and examining the thoughts associated with these feelings. By dissecting these thoughts, you can identify irrational or harmful thinking patterns and work toward developing a more balanced perspective.

Creating Your Thought Record

To create your thought record, you can use a simple table with columns. Each column will guide you through the steps to examine and challenge your thoughts:

1. **Situation**: Describe the event or moment that triggered your negative emotions. Be specific about when and where it happened (e.g., "I felt ignored during a team meeting at work on Tuesday morning.").
2. **Feelings**: Note the emotions you felt during the situation and rate their intensity on a scale of 0 to 100 (e.g., "Anxious, 70%").
3. **Automatic Thoughts**: Write down the immediate thoughts that came to your mind during the situation. These thoughts often come automatically and may be irrational or exaggerated (e.g., "Everyone thinks I'm incompetent.").
4. **Evidence Supporting These Thoughts**: List any facts or experiences that seem to justify these automatic thoughts (e.g., "I stumbled over my words during my presentation.").
5. **Evidence Against These Thoughts**: This is crucial. Identify evidence that contradicts or challenges your automatic thoughts (e.g., "I received positive feedback on my previous projects, and my question was valid.").
6. **Alternative Thoughts**: Based on the evidence against your automatic thoughts, try to come up with more balanced and rational thoughts (e.g., "Making a

mistake doesn't mean I'm incompetent. Everyone has off days.").
7. **Outcome**: Reflect on how your feelings have changed after considering alternative thoughts and again rate their intensity (e.g., "Less anxious, 30%").

Example of a Thought Record

1. **Situation:** I felt overlooked during a group get-together when attempts to join the conversation were not acknowledged.
2. **Feelings:** Embarrassed, 65%.
3. **Automatic Thoughts:** "I'm uninteresting and socially awkward."
4. **Evidence Supporting:** I felt like I couldn't find the right words to contribute effectively to the conversation.
5. **Evidence Against:** I've had engaging conversations with friends in recent days. People have complimented my sense of humor and insights before.
6. **Alternative Thoughts:** "Not every social interaction will go perfectly, and that's okay. My worth isn't measured by one awkward moment. I have qualities that are appreciated by those who know me well."
7. **Outcome:** Feeling more accepting of myself and less embarrassed, 25%.

Using Thought Records Effectively

- **Regularly practice.** The more you practice, the better you become at recognizing and challenging negative thoughts.
- **Reflect.** Regularly review your completed thought records to see your progress and patterns in thinking.
- **Be patient.** Change takes time. With consistent effort, you'll likely notice a shift toward more positive and balanced thinking.

Summary

- **Volume and Impact of Thoughts:** We have over 6,000 thoughts a day, both positive and negative. Recognizing and addressing negative thought patterns is essential for our emotional and overall well-being due to their significant impact.
- **Effects of Negative Thinking:** Negative thoughts can harm mental health, relationships, and work performance. They can worsen mental health issues and create a cycle of negativity, leading to despair, stress, anxiety, and low self-esteem.
- **Cognitive Restructuring:** This method helps shift negative thoughts to more constructive ones. It involves using thought records to document and analyze negative thoughts, promoting a positive mindset change.

- **Limiting Beliefs vs. Cognitive Distortions:** Understanding the difference between limiting beliefs (negative views on our abilities) and cognitive distortions (irrational thoughts affecting reality perception) is crucial for overcoming negativity.
- **Tools for Change:** Using cognitive restructuring and thought records can help change negative thoughts to positive ones. This process, which involves identifying, challenging, and replacing negative thoughts, improves mental health and emotional well-being.

Conclusion

In this chapter, we learned that an average person processes over 6,000 thoughts daily, many of which are negative and can significantly impact our mental health, relationships, and work. The focus was on understanding these negative thought patterns, or cognitive distortions, and providing strategies like cognitive restructuring and thought records to challenge and change them into positive ones. This approach helps improve our emotional well-being and enhances our resilience and quality of life.

Looking ahead, the next chapter will explore the concept of fear, including our fear of failure, success, and rejection. It will offer insights into viewing fear as an opportunity for growth and introduce methods to manage fear effectively. This progression from recognizing and modifying negative thoughts to embracing and managing fear marks a pivotal step toward personal development and emotional empowerment.

Chapter 4
Conquering Your Fears

Fear is the barrier to thinking outside the box.

Each of us has experienced moments when fear held us back from seizing an opportunity or pursuing a novel idea. Perhaps it was fear of failure, rejection, or even success itself that narrowed our path and dimmed the vibrant possibilities before us.

Understanding the roots of fear can help us see its physiological and psychological impacts. We will examine the subtle and overt ways fear manifests, limiting our potential and confining us to the comfort of the familiar. By confronting and understanding our fears, we can dismantle the barriers they create and unlock a world of untapped potential. Confronting your fears head-on is essential. By facing fear directly, you dismantle its power and open up new avenues for growth. Each confrontation builds resilience and helps you realize that fear doesn't have to dictate your choices.

Several years ago, I faced a decision that could redefine the trajectory of both my personal life and career. I was offered a unique opportunity to move across the country to take on a role that promised new challenges and greater responsibilities. At first, the idea was exhilarating—this was the big break I had longed for, a chance to step out of my comfort zone and prove my capabilities on a larger stage.

However, as the decision loomed closer, a familiar fear crept in, clouding my excitement with doubts and what-ifs. What if I failed spectacularly in this new role? What if I couldn't adapt to the new city or grew to regret leaving the familiarity of my current life? This fear of the unknown, of leaving behind everything comfortable and secure, began to weigh heavily on my decision-making process.

My mind was filled with scenarios of potential failure and isolation in this new setting. I found myself fixating not on the potential of what could be achieved but on everything that could go wrong. This fear almost convinced me to decline the offer, choosing the safety of my current situation over the uncertainty of a new adventure. Spending time evading fear can result in you never accomplishing anything great. When you avoid fear, you also avoid the opportunities that come with taking risks and pushing your boundaries. Embracing fear can lead to remarkable achievements and personal growth.

It was a conversation with a mentor that changed my perspective. She pointed out that fear was holding me back from expanding my horizons and that by succumbing to it, I was inadvertently stunting my personal and professional growth. "What's the worst that could happen, and how does it compare to the best that might unfold?" she asked. This simple question helped me to reframe my situation: Instead of a gamble with high risks, I began to see it as a calculated step toward growth. Confronting your fears head-on is crucial for personal growth. By facing our fears directly, we can break down the barriers they create and unlock our true potential. Avoiding fears allows them to persist and grow, but confronting them helps us build resilience and confidence.

As you read, I encourage you to reflect on your experiences with fear. Think about the times fear influenced your decision-making, affected your personal or professional growth, or changed the course of your life's journey. Make this a personal exploration of how recognizing and overcoming our fears can lead to profound personal growth and fulfillment. Together, let's learn not only to face our fears but also to harness them as tools for growth and catalysts for change.

Understanding Fear

Fear is a basic, intense emotion aroused by the detection of an imminent threat, causing immediate alarm reactions that mobilize the organism by triggering physiological changes, such as rapid heartbeat and tensing of muscles. This response is evolutionary, designed to protect organisms from potential threats to their integrity or existence, and is also known as the fear response or fight-or-flight response. It's easier to conquer your fears when you realize it doesn't have to be a life-or-death situation. Most fears are not about immediate danger but about stepping out of your comfort zone.

Reframing fear in this way can reduce its intensity and make it more manageable.

The amygdala, an almond-shaped set of nuclei in the temporal lobe of the brain, is responsible for detecting the emotional salience of stimuli and initiating the fear response, which involves preparation for motor functions involved in fight or flight, the release of stress hormones, and activation of the sympathetic nervous system (Saab & Javanbakht, 2017). Differentiating between rational and irrational fears is essential for understanding how fear affects us.

Rational fears are based on real and present dangers and invoke a fear response considered an appropriate short-term reaction to a clearly identifiable threat. For example, feeling fear when a weapon is pointed at you is rational because it signals imminent danger. Irrational fears or phobias, however, are intense fears of things that, in reality, pose little or no actual danger, and the fear response to these perceived threats is often disproportionate and persistent. Phobias are considered irrational because they lead to avoidance that can interfere with normal functioning, even though the feared object or situation is not likely to cause harm. Phobias can also severely limit a person's life by forcing changes in behavior, such as avoiding necessary medical treatments due to a fear of needles (Foy, 2023; Smith et al., 2019).

Avoid living in the past—it can tether you to old fears and regrets. Focusing on past failures or missed opportunities can prevent you from moving forward. Embrace the present moment and its potential for new experiences and growth. Fear is natural and can help individuals respond to dangers, but it can hinder them from reaching their full potential when it becomes a phobia. Understanding fear and phobias is the first step toward overcoming them, and it is important to recognize that while phobias are common, they are also treatable. With appropriate treatment and self-help strategies, you can change your mindset and learn to manage your fears and phobias effectively (Fear, 2022; Smith et al., 2019). What you resist will persist. When you try to ignore or suppress your fears, they often become more intense and pervasive. Acknowledging and addressing your fears is the first step toward overcoming them and reducing their hold on your life.

Fear of Failure

Fear of failure, also known as atychiphobia, is a complex phenomenon characterized by an intense and persistent dread of not meeting set standards or achieving personal goals. The causes of this fear are multifaceted and often deeply rooted in past experiences, such as critical upbringing, traumatic events, learned behavior, or genetics that predispose one to anxiety disorders (Fear of Failure (Atychiphobia), n.d.).

The impact of fear of failure is substantial. It can lead to low self-esteem, reduced motivation, and a tendency toward self-sabotage. Furthermore, this fear often results in a reluctance to attempt new challenges, leading to a cycle where opportunities for growth and learning are missed, and personal or professional development is hindered. This can perpetuate feelings of inadequacy and reinforce the fear of failure that is being avoided.

Examples of how fear of failure may manifest in your life include:

- **Avoidance of Risk:** Choosing not to apply for a job or promotion due to the belief that rejection is inevitable.
- **Procrastination:** Delaying starting a project due to a belief that it won't be successful, thus not giving it the full effort it deserves.
- **Self-Deprecating Predictions:** Telling others they will likely fail to lower their expectations.
- **Physical Symptoms:** Experiencing physical symptoms like headaches or nausea that conveniently prevent one from facing a challenging task.
- **Perfectionism:** Setting unrealistically high standards and being overly critical of oneself when those standards are not met (Winch, 2013).

Fear of Success

Fear of success might seem counterintuitive since success is generally seen as a positive outcome. However, for many, the prospect of achieving success brings anxiety and a multitude of unintended consequences that might not be immediately apparent. Fear of success, also known as success anxiety or achievemephobia, revolves around the worry that success will alter one's life in ways that are not manageable or desirable (Pietrangelo, 2020).

The underlying causes of fear of success are multifaceted and deeply rooted in psychological responses to change and expectations. Often, individuals fear the increased responsibilities, the potential isolation from peers, and the heightened scrutiny that success can bring (Rozen, n.d.). For some, childhood experiences such as being punished for standing out or early failures can instill a long-lasting aversion to success. Cultural factors like backlash avoidance, where individuals, particularly women, face negative reactions when they succeed, also play a significant role.

Identifying fear of success can be challenging as it often masquerades as other anxieties or behavioral patterns. Common signs include:

- **Procrastination**: Delaying tasks to avoid potential success
- **Self-Sabotage**: Engaging in behaviors that undermine one's success, such as substance abuse or quitting projects prematurely
- **Perfectionism**: Setting unattainably high standards that are impossible to meet, thus providing an excuse to give up (Pietrangelo, 2020)
- **Low Goal Setting**: Avoiding setting goals that challenge one's abilities or that could lead to significant progress (Cherry, 2023)

Fear of Rejection

The fear of rejection, also known as anthropophobia, manifests as a dread of not being accepted by others, including fear of disapproval over one's appearance, actions, or mere presence. This fear is primal and deeply embedded in our instinct to survive by belonging to a group; historically, being ostracized meant a literal threat to one's survival (Luna, 2018). Consider someone who, despite feeling unfulfilled, stays in a relationship because perhaps the fear of being alone and rejected by others is too daunting.

The root of this fear often lies in a deep-seated need for acceptance and belonging. People fear rejection because it can confirm their worst fears about themselves—being unlovable, inadequate, or fundamentally flawed. This fear can be exacerbated by past traumas, such as childhood abandonment or continual negative feedback, which cement feelings of unworthiness (Peer, 2020).

The fear of rejection can manifest in various ways, affecting all areas of one's life:

- **Hesitance to Express Opinions**: Avoiding sharing one's thoughts for fear of judgment.
- **People-Pleasing**: Engaging in behaviors to gain approval and avoid conflict.
- **Sensitivity to Criticism**: Viewing criticism as a personal attack rather than constructive feedback.
- **Avoidance of Risks**: Shying away from new relationships or opportunities due to fear of failure or rejection (Peer, 2020).

Reframing Fear as Opportunity

In confronting the fears that paralyze us—whether fear of failure, rejection, or the unknown—we need to adopt a mindset that views these experiences as opportunities for growth and learning instead of obstacles. This isn't just positive thinking; it requires a fundamental shift in how we understand and interact with the world (Anthony, 2016).

Every setback or rejection can carry a lesson. Rather than seeing these experiences as a reflection of our worth, we can view them as valuable feedback. This shift in perspective allows us to gently detach our self-esteem from any outcomes and focus on what can be learned. For example, a breakup or a strained relationship can provide insights into our communication styles, emotional needs, or compatibility issues, offering a clearer understanding of what we truly seek in a partner.

The Power of Cognitive Restructuring

In the context of reframing fear, cognitive restructuring allows you to dissect your fears analytically. Often, your fears are based on distorted perceptions that can be deconstructed and viewed more rationally. For instance, your fear of public speaking might be rooted in exaggerated assumptions about the negative outcomes of making a mistake. Cognitive restructuring helps by challenging these assumptions, prompting you to question the validity and probability of your feared outcomes. You can shift from a mindset that views public speaking as a threatening event to one that sees it as a chance to improve your speaking skills and gain confidence. This shift diminishes the initial fear and encourages a more adaptive and proactive approach to your personal and professional challenges.

The Role of Effort and Practice

It's not an instantaneous shift but a gradual process of building resilience. Transforming fear into opportunity requires consistent effort and practice. By regularly exposing ourselves to our fears in controlled and manageable ways, we can desensitize ourselves to the anxiety they produce and build confidence in our ability to handle them.

Fear as a Precursor to Excitement

It's helpful to remember that physiologically, fear and excitement share many symptoms: a racing heart, heightened senses, and an adrenaline rush. By mentally rebranding our fear as pre-performance excitement, we position ourselves to harness this energy positively. This rebranding can transform daunting tasks—like public speaking or setting a boundary with someone—into exhilarating opportunities that propel us forward.

Lessons of Failure: Reflective Prompts for Growth

In this section, we invite you to delve into your past experiences of failures and rejections. We've designed five thoughtful prompts to guide you in reflecting on these moments and extracting valuable lessons to enhance your personal and professional growth. Remember that you can use the blank pages at the end of this book to journal your responses. You can also use a notebook or even your phone. By engaging with these prompts in the way that is most accessible to you, you'll gain insights that can empower you to navigate future challenges more effectively.

Turning Setbacks into Setups: View each failure not as a setback but as a setup for future success. Remember, failures are simply feedback, guiding you toward better strategies and stronger resilience.

- Think of a time when a failure turned out to be an opportunity. How can you apply this perspective to your current challenges?

Growth Mindset vs. Fixed Mindset: Embrace a growth mindset to transform your fear into opportunity. This approach encourages you to welcome challenges, persist through setbacks, learn from criticism, and find inspiration in others' successes. Compare this with a fixed mindset, which sees skills as unchangeable and often leads to a fear of failure, stifling growth and opportunity.

- Reflect on a situation where you faced a challenge. Did you approach it with a growth mindset or a fixed mindset? How did this impact the outcome?

The Power of Positive Reframing: Changing your negative thought patterns about fear can transform it from a barrier into a motivator, empowering you to face challenges with a new perspective.

- Identify a recent fear or failure. How can you reframe your thoughts about it to see it as a motivator rather than a barrier?

Fear as a Precursor to Action: Use fear as a catalyst for action. These strategies can help build your confidence and reduce the impact of fear, turning it into a powerful motivator instead of a blockade.

- What small, achievable goals can you set to confront a fear you have? How can seeking support help you take the first steps?

Celebrating Small Wins: Make it a habit to acknowledge and celebrate each small victory on your journey. This practice helps shift your focus from what's going wrong to what's going right, reinforcing the positive aspects of your efforts and building momentum that can make fear less daunting.

- What small victories have you achieved recently? How did celebrating these wins impact your motivation and confidence?

Managing Your Fear in the Moment

In moments of fear, you can improve your ability to manage stress and anxiety effectively. This proactive approach allows you to feel more empowered and less overwhelmed in fearful situations.

Remember the power of positive self-talk. Remind yourself that you are in control, that you are calm, and that you can handle the situation. Positive affirmations can reframe your mindset and reduce the intensity of fear.

Diaphragmatic Breathing

Diaphragmatic breathing, or belly breathing, is a powerful method to reduce anxiety and promote calmness. This technique involves engaging the diaphragm to take deep breaths, which can help slow your heart rate and stabilize blood pressure, contributing to overall relaxation.

How to Do It:

1. Lie down or sit comfortably with your shoulders relaxed.
2. Place one hand on your chest and the other on your belly.
3. Breathe in slowly through your nose, ensuring your belly moves out against your hand more than your chest does.
4. Exhale slowly through pursed lips, tightening your abdominal muscles to help expel air (Johnson, 2020).

Guided Imagery

Guided imagery is a mental escape that involves envisioning a calm, peaceful setting or event using all five senses. This technique can help redirect your thoughts from anxiety and stress to tranquility and peace.

How to Do It:

1. Find a quiet place to relax and close your eyes.
2. Picture a serene setting—imagine the sights, sounds, smells, and textures. For example, visualize walking on a beach, hearing the waves, smelling the ocean, and feeling the sand under your feet.
3. Focus on this scene for several minutes, breathing slowly and deeply as you do so (Cuncic, 2023).

Simple Stretches

Engaging in simple stretches can help relieve physical tension, which often accompanies fear and anxiety. These stretches can be done almost anywhere and require only a few minutes.

Stretches to Try:

- **Seated Spinal Twist:** While seated, turn your torso to the right, holding the back of your chair for support. Hold for a few seconds, then switch to the left.

- **Chest Opener Stretch:** Interlock your fingers behind your head and gently push your chest forward, drawing your elbows back. This opens up the chest and stretches the shoulder muscles.
- **Neck Rotation:** Gently rotate your neck clockwise and then counterclockwise to relieve neck tension. This can be done while seated or standing (Migala, 2023).

Summary

- **Understanding Fear as a Barrier**: Fear, whether of failure, rejection, or success, can significantly limit our ability to think innovatively and seize opportunities. It often prevents us from stepping out of our comfort zones and embracing potential growth opportunities.
- **Physiological and Psychological Impacts**: Fear triggers a physiological response that can be paralyzing, but understanding the roots of this emotion—whether rational or irrational—can help us manage its effects more effectively.
- **Fear of Failure and Success**: Both fears are deeply rooted in past experiences and societal expectations. Fear of failure leads to avoidance of risks and missed opportunities, while fear of success can cause anxiety about the changes and responsibilities that come with success.
- **Reframing Fear as Opportunity**: By shifting our perspective on fear from an obstacle to a catalyst for growth, we can transform experiences of fear into opportunities for learning and personal development.

- **Practical Techniques to Manage Fear**: Techniques like cognitive restructuring, diaphragmatic breathing, and guided imagery help manage and reduce the impact of fear, enabling individuals to face challenging situations with confidence and calmness.

Conclusion

By confronting our fears—whether they arise from concerns about failure, rejection, or even success—we can start to break them down. This chapter has drawn on personal anecdotes and scientific research to illustrate how fear can restrict our potential by anchoring us to what is familiar and comfortable. Recognizing these barriers can be challenging, but it is certainly achievable. As we have discovered, each fear has the potential to either restrict us or propel our personal and professional growth forward.

As you turn the page, I encourage you to reflect on your patterns of self-sabotage. Think about how the fears you've faced may be shaping these behaviors. The upcoming chapter continues our exploration of fear by examining common self-sabotaging behaviors such as procrastination, perfectionism, and people-pleasing. These behaviors are often driven by the fears we've discussed and serve as mechanisms that hold us back from realizing our full potential. We will see how cultivating self-compassion can effectively counter these tendencies, enabling us to transcend our self-imposed limits.

Help Someone Create a Better Future

"The view you adopt for yourself profoundly affects the way you lead your life. It can determine whether you become the person you want to be."

— Carol Dweck

When life throws a big curveball at you—we're talking a real whip, flying at over 80mph directly in the face of your calm existence—you have two choices. You can either decide that by hook or by crook, you will evade as many curveballs as you can, or you can head on to the field, find a Babe Ruth-level mentor, and play, play, play!

I wrote this book to help you make that choice—the choice to be a doer. You see, as hard as you try, you can't shy away from pain, disappointment, or loss. However, a strong yet flexible mindset allows you to utilize your biggest losses to refine your process, understand your triggers, and respond instead of react to tough situations. It allows you to find meaning from pain and bring a better, kinder, more empathetic self to the people who surround you.

You have seen how limiting beliefs can lead you to make harmful choices and discovered how reframing your thoughts can enable you to make wise, evidence-backed decisions that will help you be more productive. You have also seen how to transform fear—arguably the biggest single enemy of success—into a superpower that propels you forward far more effectively than you may have imagined. I hope that by now, you know the extent to which your reality is shaped by how you choose to see it. If so, I hope I can ask you for a quick favor.

By leaving a review of this book on Amazon, you'll help new readers find proven, effective strategies that will empower them to embrace a positive mindset.

Thank you so much. It will only take a line or two to let others know what they can find within these pages. I hope you enjoy the rest of your read... the best is yet to come!

Click the link or scan the QR code below to leave your review on Amazon

https://www.amazon.com/review/create-review/?asin=B0DG86N7QB

Chapter 5

Escaping the Grip of Self-Sabotage

On *Friends*, Rachel Green has an opportunity for a career in fashion, which has been her dream. However, when offered a job in Paris, she initially decides to stay in New York because of her fear of losing her current relationships and the comfort of her existing life.

She nearly misses out on a major career opportunity and the chance to fulfill her long-term professional ambitions. Although she eventually decides to take the job, her indecision illustrates how fear of change and leaving one's comfort zone can lead to self-sabotage.

Or consider Walter White—a high school chemistry teacher turned methamphetamine manufacturing drug dealer on *Breaking Bad*, who repeatedly sabotages his chances to leave the criminal life. Despite multiple opportunities to secure his family's future and walk away safely, his pride and need for control drive him to make increasingly dangerous choices.

His decisions lead to severe personal and familial destruction, showing how his inability to relinquish control and his pride directly sabotage his initial intentions of securing his family's future.

These two examples illustrate how self-sabotage can manifest and deeply impact one's career and personal life. These narratives serve as mirrors reflecting some of our fears, insecurities, and misplaced priorities. Whether it's fear of leaving your comfort zone, like Rachel, or a compulsive need for control, as seen in Walter, these behaviors can significantly impede our growth and happiness.

Our decisions can have far-reaching consequences, often shaping the trajectory of our personal and professional lives. For example, staying in a comfort zone might protect us from immediate discomfort, but it can also prevent us from achieving our full potential. Each decision, no matter how small, can lead to significant outcomes. Recognizing the weight of our choices can motivate us to make decisions that align with our long-term goals and well-being.

As you read this chapter, reflect on your own experiences. Do you see elements of Rachel's hesitance or Walter's pride in your life decisions? How have these moments influenced your personal and professional trajectories? Perhaps you pull away in relationships due to past criticism about being too dependent. You may skip training sessions when they get tough, using excuses like being too busy or tired or bad weather. Recognizing these patterns is the first step toward overcoming the self-sabotage that may be holding you back from achieving your full potential.

Cutting the cord on self-sabotaging behaviors requires a commitment to standing up to your inner critic and making deliberate changes. This might involve breaking away from unhealthy patterns, setting boundaries, or asserting your needs and desires. Standing up to yourself means acknowledging your worth and refusing to let fear or past failures dictate your future. By taking control and making proactive decisions, you can overcome the grip of self-sabotage and pave the way for personal growth and success.

Understanding Self-Sabotage

Self-sabotage involves behaviors or thought patterns that deliberately or unconsciously hinder a person's progress, happiness, or success. Despite their intentions or desires, individuals often engage in self-sabotage, which can manifest in various aspects of their lives, such as relationships, careers, and personal growth.

Root Causes of Self-Sabotage

Self-sabotage is a complex phenomenon with multiple contributing factors, often rooted in psychological elements. Here are some critical causes:

- **Fear**: Many engage in self-sabotage due to fear of failure or success. This fear can stem from past experiences or ingrained beliefs about their capabilities.

- **Low Self-Esteem**: People with low self-esteem may feel undeserving of success. Their negative self-image often leads to behaviors confirming their self-doubts, ultimately sabotaging their efforts.
- **Need for Control**: In uncertain situations, some prefer to control the outcome by ensuring failure, which, paradoxically, is more comfortable than facing unpredictable success.
- **Childhood Trauma**: Early experiences of neglect, criticism, or lack of support can lead to patterns of self-sabotage. Individuals might carry forward a belief that they are inadequate, shaping their adult behaviors and relationships (French, 2023).

Recognizing Self-Sabotage

Identifying self-sabotaging behavior is the first step toward change. Common signs include:

- Procrastination or avoiding tasks that lead to progress
- Engaging in negative self-talk or doubting one's abilities incessantly
- Sabotaging relationships through distrust or fear of intimacy (Field, 2023)
- Overcommitting or perfectionism, which sets one up for failure or burnout

Overcoming Self-Sabotage

Breaking the cycle of self-sabotage requires awareness, understanding, and proactive strategies:

- **Self-Awareness**: Recognizing and acknowledging self-sabotaging patterns is crucial. Reflection and self-monitoring can help identify what triggers these behaviors.
- **Setting Realistic Goals**: Small, manageable goals can prevent the overwhelm that leads to procrastination and self-sabotage. Celebrating small victories builds confidence and reinforces positive behaviors.
- **Seeking Professional Help**: Therapy, particularly cognitive behavioral therapy (CBT), can be effective in addressing the underlying beliefs and fears that fuel self-sabotage.
- **Building Healthy Relationships**: Developing supportive and understanding relationships can provide the encouragement and feedback necessary to overcome self-sabotaging behaviors.

Consequences of Self-Sabotage

Self-sabotage can deeply affect your personal and professional well-being across various aspects of your life.

Emotional Consequences

When you engage in self-sabotage, you may find yourself trapped in a cycle of negative emotions such as guilt, shame, and low self-esteem. These feelings often arise when you recognize your self-destructive behaviors but feel powerless to change them. For instance, you might know that procrastination harms your goals, yet you continue to delay essential tasks, leading to feelings of failure and self-reproach.

Impact on Relationships

Self-sabotage can severely damage both personal and professional relationships. In romantic relationships, actions like unjustified jealousy, excessive criticism, or creating unnecessary conflicts can destroy trust and intimacy, often resulting in breakups or divorce. Similarly, in friendships and family dynamics, self-sabotage may lead you to withdraw from loved ones or fail to meet commitments, straining these relationships and potentially leading to isolation.

Professional Repercussions

Self-sabotage can block your career progression at work. Behaviors such as missing deadlines, undermining your ideas during meetings, or avoiding promotions due to fear of rejection can stall your professional growth and lead to job dissatisfaction and stress.

Academic Underachievement

As a student, self-sabotage might manifest as poor study habits, skipping classes, or neglecting to turn in assignments, leading to failing grades and limiting your future educational and career opportunities.

Physical Health Impacts

Ongoing self-sabotage can lead to chronic stress, resulting in physical health issues such as insomnia, headaches, digestive problems, and a weakened immune system. Over time, this stress may contribute to more serious health problems like heart disease and hypertension.

Wider Life Implications

More broadly, self-sabotage can prevent you from achieving your life goals and reaching your full potential. It may show up as financial instability due to impulsive spending, poor investment choices, or inadequate savings. Additionally, it can lead to unhealthy coping mechanisms like substance abuse, further worsening the negative impact on your quality of life (Perry, 2022; *Self-Sabotaging*, 2023).

Common Self-Sabotaging Behaviors

We engage in self-sabotaging behaviors because they offer a misguided sense of comfort and control in the face of fear and uncertainty. Despite our best intentions, common self-sabotaging behaviors can subtly undermine our efforts to succeed and thrive. From procrastination to perfectionism, these patterns manifest in various ways, each acting as a barrier to our personal and professional growth. It's often our internal battles that prove to be the greatest challenges.

Procrastination

Procrastination is delaying or putting off tasks until the last minute or past the deadline despite knowing there could be negative consequences. This behavior is often a form of self-regulation failure, where you don't perform tasks at the necessary time, leading to increased stress and clutter in your personal and professional life (Cherry, 2022c).

Tips for Overcoming Procrastination

To combat procrastination and start managing your tasks more effectively, consider these strategies:

- **Identify what triggers your procrastination.** Recognize the situations and emotional states that make you more likely to procrastinate. Is it fear of failure, perfectionism, or perhaps feeling overwhelmed by a task? Understanding these triggers can help you develop strategies to counter them.
- **Prioritize tasks.** List your tasks in order of importance and tackle them accordingly. This helps ensure you complete what's most important first and not just what you feel like doing. It can be helpful to use tools like calendars or to-do lists to keep track of deadlines and priorities.
- **Manage distractions.** Identify what commonly distracts you from your work and take steps to reduce these interruptions. This might mean turning off notifications on your phone, finding a quieter workplace, or setting specific times when you are unavailable to others.

- **Break tasks into smaller chunks**. Large tasks can seem daunting and exacerbate procrastination. Break them into smaller, more manageable parts. This approach makes the task seem less overwhelming and allows you to feel progress as you complete each smaller section, which can be motivating.
- **Set realistic deadlines**. Give yourself enough time to complete tasks by setting realistic deadlines. If you underestimate the time required, you might rush and feel stressed, which can lead to procrastination.
- **Reward yourself**. Set up a reward system for when you complete a task or a portion of it. This could be something small like taking a break to walk outside, enjoying a snack, or watching a short video. Rewards can make completing tasks more satisfying and motivate you to keep moving forward (*Why You Procrastinate and How to Stop*, 2022).

Perfectionism

Perfectionism is a personality trait characterized by setting extremely high and often unattainable standards for oneself and sometimes for others. While it can drive people to achieve great things, it often comes with a cost to mental and emotional well-being. Perfectionism is associated with various problems, including stress, anxiety, and depression, and it affects how people manage their personal and professional lives (Dorwart, 2023).

Tips for Overcoming Perfectionism

If you're struggling with perfectionism, here are some strategies that can help:

- **Identify perfectionistic tendencies.** Start by recognizing the situations where your perfectionism surfaces. This could be at work, during hobbies, or in personal relationships. Understanding when and how you display perfectionistic behaviors is the first step in managing them.
- **Allow for imperfection.** Understand that making mistakes is a part of being human. Instead of striving for perfection, aim for progress. Embrace mistakes as learning opportunities and realize they do not define your worth or capabilities.
- **Develop reasonable standards and expectations.** Set achievable goals based on realistic standards rather than idealized outcomes. This involves adjusting your benchmarks for success and acknowledging that "good enough" is often sufficient for most tasks.
- **Break down tasks.** Instead of approaching a large project with an all-or-nothing mindset, break it down into manageable parts. This makes the task seem less daunting and helps to reduce the pressure to perform perfectly. Celebrate small achievements along the way to maintain motivation and perspective.
- **Challenge negative self-talk.** Be mindful of how you talk to yourself, especially after perceived failures or mistakes. Replace harsh criticism with

more compassionate and supportive dialogue. This shift in mindset can reduce feelings of low self-esteem that often accompany perfectionistic tendencies.
- **Embrace a growth mindset.** Focus on personal development and continuous improvement rather than flawless performance. View challenges as opportunities to learn and grow rather than threats to your self-worth.
- **Seek professional help if needed.** If perfectionism is deeply ingrained and affecting your quality of life, consider talking to a mental health professional. CBT is particularly effective in addressing the thought patterns associated with perfectionism (Cox, 2022).

People-Pleasing

People-pleasing refers to the tendency to prioritize others' happiness and approval over your own needs, often at the expense of your well-being. This behavior is typically driven by the desire to avoid conflict and be liked by others, which can lead to a cycle of neglecting your needs and desires.

Tips for Overcoming People-Pleasing

If you recognize yourself as a people-pleaser and want to change this pattern, consider these practical steps:

- **Set boundaries.** Learn to say no when requests conflict with your priorities or well-being. Setting boundaries is crucial for mental health and helps others understand your limits and respect your time.

- **Prioritize your needs.** Make sure to prioritize your needs and schedule time for activities that fulfill you personally and professionally. Remember, taking care of yourself is not selfish; it's necessary.
- **Stop over-apologizing.** People-pleasers often apologize to avoid conflict or disapproval even when they haven't done anything wrong. Work on being mindful of when and why you apologize and try to limit apologies to when you truly owe them.
- **Give yourself time to decide.** When asked for a favor or to make a decision, take your time to think about whether it's something you really want to do or if you're just trying to please someone else. This helps you make decisions that are true to your own interests and limits.
- **Embrace discomfort.** Saying no or setting boundaries can feel uncomfortable at first, especially if you're not used to it. Recognize that the discomfort is a part of growth, and it will decrease as you become more accustomed to asserting yourself.

Nurturing Self-Compassion

Self-compassion means treating yourself with the same kindness, concern, and support you'd typically extend to a good friend. It's about recognizing that suffering, failure, and imperfection are part of the human experience (Van Edwards, 2021). When you make a mistake or encounter a challenging situation, self-compassion allows you to deal with your feelings with understanding and patience instead of berating yourself.

Examples of Self-Compassion in Action

- **Acknowledging Your Struggles without Judgment**: For instance, if you fail to meet a work deadline, instead of criticizing yourself as incompetent, you might say, "I'm disappointed I didn't finish on time, but I understand that I had a lot on my plate. I'll plan better next time."
- **Offering Yourself Comfort**: Suppose you're feeling down because of a personal setback. Rather than ignoring your emotions or telling yourself to "get over it," you might treat yourself to a relaxing night in, watch your favorite movie, or engage in another nurturing activity.

Benefits of Self-Compassion

Practicing self-compassion can significantly counteract self-sabotaging behaviors and promote a growth mindset. Here's how:

- **Reduces Negative Self-Talk**: By cultivating self-compassion, you're less likely to fall into despair and self-criticism when things go wrong. This shift can decrease anxiety and depression, improving your overall emotional resilience.
- **Encourages a Growth Mindset**: With self-compassion, failures are seen as opportunities to learn and grow rather than as reflections of your worth. This perspective fosters a growth mindset,

which enhances your willingness to embrace challenges and persist in the face of setbacks.
- **Enhances Well-Being**: Self-compassion leads to better emotional recovery and less reactivity to negative events. It helps soothe the nervous system, reducing the likelihood of stress responses that can exacerbate physical and mental health issues (Coelho & Smith, 2013).

Integrating Self-Compassion into Daily Life

By embracing self-compassion, you shield yourself from the harmful effects of self-sabotage and open the door to a more accepting and fulfilling relationship with yourself. This foundation of self-kindness is crucial for sustainable personal growth and well-being.

- **Mindfulness**: Be present with your feelings without judgment. Notice when you're self-critical and gently redirect your thoughts to more compassionate responses.
- **Common Humanity**: Remind yourself that you're not alone in your struggles. Everyone faces challenges and makes mistakes (Ladouceur, n.d.).
- **Self-Kindness**: Actively soothe yourself when distressed. This might involve speaking to yourself kindly or engaging in self-care practices that affirm your worth and comfort your psyche.

Practical Strategies for Cultivating Self-Compassion

- **Cultivate acceptance.** Embracing acceptance involves acknowledging your feelings without judgment and accepting your current state of mind. This means not forcing change but allowing yourself to be where you are, recognizing that this state is part of the human experience.
- **Forgive yourself.** Self-forgiveness is crucial for overcoming guilt and moving forward. It involves recognizing mistakes and missteps as part of being human and allowing yourself to step forward without ongoing self-punishment. This is key to healing and maintaining a compassionate view of oneself.
- **Comfort your body.** Physical self-care can be a form of self-compassion. This might include activities like taking a warm bath, engaging in gentle exercise, or getting enough sleep. Comforting your body helps to soothe your mind and reinforce a caring attitude toward yourself.
- **Take self-compassion breaks.** During stressful moments, pause and offer yourself kindness and acknowledgment. Place a hand over your heart or simply close your eyes and speak gently to yourself, affirming that it's okay to feel how you do and reminding yourself of your common humanity.
- **Practice loving-kindness meditation.** This meditation focuses on developing feelings of goodwill, kindness, and warmth toward oneself and others, thereby enhancing one's capacity for self-compassion.

- **Keep a self-compassion journal.** Writing in a journal can help you process emotions and reflect on your experiences with a compassionate mindset. Regularly journaling can also help you track your progress in cultivating self-compassion and recognize patterns that need more attention.
- **Express gratitude.** Gratitude shifts your focus from what's wrong to right, helping to counteract the negativity bias and promote a more compassionate outlook toward life's experiences. Keeping a gratitude journal or simply mentally acknowledging things you are grateful for can bolster self-compassion.
- **Treat yourself as you'd treat a friend.** Apply the kindness, understanding, and support you'd offer a friend to yourself. When you catch yourself being self-critical, ask, "Would I talk to a friend this way?" This helps align your self-dialogue with a more compassionate tone.
- **Celebrate your small accomplishments.** Recognizing and celebrating even the minor victories can boost your self-esteem and reinforce positive self-regard. This helps build a sense of efficacy and personal worth, which are critical to self-compassion.
- **Reach out when you need help.** Asking for help is a strong act of self-compassion. It acknowledges your limits and emphasizes your worthiness of support. This can strengthen your connections with others and help build a support system that fosters further self-compassion (Brooten-Brooks, 2022; Moore, 2019).

Summary

- **Understanding Self-Sabotage**: Self-sabotage involves behaviors or thought patterns that hinder one's progress, happiness, or success. It often stems from fear, low self-esteem, a need for control, or childhood trauma, leading individuals to deliberately or unconsciously block their efforts.
- **Recognizing Self-Sabotage**: Identifying self-sabotaging behavior is crucial. Common signs include procrastination, negative self-talk, sabotaging relationships, and perfectionism. Being aware of these behaviors is the first step toward overcoming them.
- **Overcoming Self-Sabotage**: To break the cycle, practice self-awareness, set realistic goals, and seek professional help if needed. Building healthy relationships can also provide necessary support and feedback to counter self-sabotaging behaviors.
- **Consequences of Self-Sabotage**: Self-sabotage can have widespread effects on emotional well-being, relationships, professional life, academic achievement, and physical health. Understanding these consequences can motivate individuals to address and change their self-sabotaging behaviors.
- **Practical Strategies for Change**: Some effective strategies include cultivating self-compassion, setting boundaries, prioritizing tasks, and embracing a growth mindset. These approaches can help individuals manage their self-sabotage and achieve personal and professional fulfillment.

Conclusion

As we've learned, self-sabotage stems from various psychological factors, including fear, low self-esteem, and the lingering effects of childhood trauma. These underlying issues can lead us to procrastinate, engage in negative self-talk, and ultimately hinder our progress. Recognizing these patterns is the first step toward overcoming the barriers we often set for ourselves.

In the next section, we'll explore the transformative power of adopting a growth mindset. We'll move into Part III to examine how fixed mindset patterns contribute to imposter syndrome and the strategies we can employ to cultivate resilience and a more fulfilling approach to our challenges. Prepare to discover how changing your mindset can enhance your personal and professional life and enable you to embrace and overcome the hurdles that come your way.

Part 3
Nurturing a Mindset for Success

Chapter 6
Cultivating A Growth Mindset

 "Becoming is better than being."

— Carol Dweck

In a growth mindset, the emphasis is on "becoming"—the ongoing process of learning, evolving, and transcending previous limits. Unlike a fixed mindset, which is inherently tied to the notion of static abilities and inherent talents, a growth mindset thrives on the belief that abilities can be developed through dedication and hard work. This approach does not just apply to acquiring new skills but also involves deepening your understanding, enhancing your creativity, and overcoming challenges in your life.

In her influential research, psychologist Carol Dweck introduced the concepts of fixed and growth mindsets, offering a new understanding of how your beliefs about your abilities can shape your life (Carol Dweck: Thinker, n.d.). The impact of

Dweck's philosophy is significant: By focusing on "becoming," you can embrace a life of continuous learning and resilience. You can see every setback as a setup for a comeback and redefine failures as opportunities for growth. This perspective frees you from the fear of not being good enough and fuels your journey toward mastery and self-improvement.

In this chapter, we will explore how the principles of "becoming" can transform your approach to life's challenges, enhance your ability to adapt and innovate, and ultimately lead to greater satisfaction and achievement. By the end of this chapter, you should understand the significance of prioritizing "becoming" over "being" and feel equipped to apply this transformative outlook to various aspects of your life, fostering a more fulfilling and progressive journey.

Why Growth Mindset Matters

Dweck's research highlights that believing in the potential to develop your abilities—not merely relying on raw talent or innate intelligence—can lead to greater achievements. While a fixed mindset might limit you to your initial capabilities, a growth mindset welcomes challenges and sees failures not as insurmountable setbacks but as opportunities for growth and learning. Understanding the importance of a growth mindset starts with recognizing how your mental approach to learning and facing challenges can profoundly shape your experiences and outcomes.

Take, for example, the brilliant inventor Thomas Edison as a prime example of someone with a growth mindset., His relentless pursuit of innovation led to groundbreaking inventions like the electric light bulb, phonograph, and motion picture camera. Despite facing numerous failures, Edison did not view these setbacks as defeats but as vital steps in the learning process. He famously said, "I have not failed. I've just found 10,000 ways that won't work." This epitomizes the growth mindset—the belief that each failure is a chance to learn and improve.

This mindset nurtures resilience, encouraging you to push through difficulties with the understanding that effort and time can culminate in mastery and success. Dweck's studies, especially those involving students, have shown that individuals who embrace a growth mindset generally perform better over time as they persist in learning and developing new skills instead of stalling.

The benefits of fostering a growth mindset go beyond academic or professional success; it's also about personal development and the satisfaction of continuously expanding your horizons and capabilities. With a growth mindset, you're more likely to seek and excel in challenging situations, leading to a more fulfilling and engaging life.

Change is often met with resistance due to fear of the unknown and discomfort with leaving familiar territory. However, viewing change as an opportunity for growth and learning can transform this apprehension into excitement. Embracing change means being open to new experiences, adapting to different circumstances, and continuously seeking improvement. This adaptability enhances personal and professional development and fosters resilience in the face of life's inevitable uncertainties.

Reclaiming your freedom is a crucial aspect of adopting a growth mindset. It involves breaking free from the constraints of self-imposed limitations and societal expectations. By embracing the idea that you can continually grow and improve, you liberate yourself from the fear of failure and the pressure to conform to fixed abilities. This newfound freedom allows you to pursue your passions and interests with vigor and confidence, knowing that your potential is not static but ever-expanding.

Harnessing a Growth Mindset

Embracing a growth mindset extends beyond just academic or professional achievements; it profoundly impacts all aspects of your life, including your education, career, relationships, and personal growth. This adaptable mindset equips you with the resilience needed to overcome challenges and achieve your goals in these areas.

In your educational journey, adopting a growth mindset means approaching learning with enthusiasm and perseverance. You'll start seeing challenges as opportunities to broaden your knowledge and skills, enhancing your learning outcomes and leading to greater academic success. This mindset prepares you for lifelong learning, which is crucial in our ever-evolving world (*Growth Mindset*, 2024).

Professionally, a growth mindset can significantly boost your career progression. If you cultivate this mindset, you're more likely to seek feedback, embrace new challenges, and learn from failures, all of which drive innovation and efficiency at work. Such a proactive attitude is highly prized in modern workplaces, where adaptability and ongoing learning are key to success.

In terms of relationships, the principles of a growth mindset—like open communication, empathy, and the belief that effort leads to improvement—help you build stronger, more supportive connections. By viewing conflicts as opportunities to strengthen your bonds, you can improve your interpersonal skills and deepen your relationships (*Mastering Love*, 2023).

Lastly, on a personal level, embracing a growth mindset encourages you to continuously seek self-improvement. It inspires you to set higher personal standards, acquire new skills, and step out of your comfort zone, leading to a more fulfilling and enriched life.

The Consequences of Fixed Mindset Patterns

A fixed mindset begins to take root early in our lives, shaped by experiences, upbringing, and even the subtle cues we receive from those around us. This mindset, characterized by the belief that our abilities, intelligence, and talents are static and unchangeable, profoundly impacts our approach to challenges and learning.

Signs and Behaviors of a Fixed Mindset

If you have a fixed mindset, you might often hesitate before taking on challenges, show a heightened sensitivity to criticism, and give up easily when faced with obstacles. You might attribute your success to inherent talent rather than effort and view failures as insurmountable reflections of your abilities.

This perspective fosters a fear of failure, leading you to avoid risks that could lead to growth (*Fixed Mindset*, 2023).

Leaders who embrace a growth mindset prioritize the process over solely concentrating on the outcome. They believe that attributes such as intelligence and talent can be cultivated with time. Conversely, leaders with a fixed mindset are excessively focused on results and may be resistant to change. The mindset one adopts can greatly influence their effectiveness and success in leadership roles.

Implications for Personal Growth and Success

The consequences of a fixed mindset extend far into personal and professional lives. For example, consider a professional who avoids taking on new responsibilities or learning new skills because they doubt their capability to succeed beyond their current abilities. This stifles their career growth and limits their potential contributions to their organization (*Fixed Mindset*, 2021).

In another scenario, a student might shy away from challenging academic subjects, convinced of their unchangeable limitations in certain areas. This impedes their intellectual growth and diminishes their confidence, creating a cycle of doubt and underachievement.

Reflection and Journaling

To counteract the negative implications of a fixed mindset, reflect on your upbringing and past experiences that may have contributed to this mindset. Understanding the origins can be your first step toward transformation. I encourage you to use the blank pages at the end of this book for journaling about your personal experiences with a fixed mindset and to actively plan steps toward embracing a growth mindset. This practice can help you recognize and overcome the limitations of a fixed mindset, fostering a new path toward personal growth and success. By understanding and addressing these patterns, you can break free from the constraints of a fixed mindset, unlocking a fuller, more successful version of yourself.

Fixed Mindset and Imposter Syndrome

Imposter syndrome is the internal experience of believing you are not as competent as others perceive you to be. Despite evidence of success, individuals with imposter syndrome attribute their accomplishments to luck or timing rather than their effort and abilities. This phenomenon is not considered a clinical disorder but is a widespread psychological pattern that can affect anyone, particularly high achievers and perfectionists.

Characteristics and Symptoms

Common symptoms of imposter syndrome include persistent self-doubt, a sense of being a fraud, fear of not meeting expectations, and undermining one's achievements. Individuals may feel they don't truly belong in their roles or deserve their successes, fearing eventual exposure as a fraud (*Imposter Syndrome*, 2022; Saymeh, 2023).

Imposter Syndrome as a Manifestation of Fixed Mindset

Imposter syndrome is closely tied to a fixed mindset. A fixed mindset, where individuals believe their abilities are static, sets the stage for imposter feelings. In this mindset, successes are not internalized as evidence of capability but are seen as flukes. This aligns with the imposter syndrome, where individuals feel an internal lack of worthiness and competencedespite external achievements.

The Self-Sabotage Connection

Imposter syndrome leads to self-sabotage, as the fear of being "found out" can prevent individuals from pursuing opportunities that could lead to recognition and further success. It creates a cycle where the fear of failure prevents taking risks necessary for growth, reinforcing the belief in one's inadequacy (Cuncic, 2022).

Overcoming Imposter Syndrome with a Growth Mindset

Imposter syndrome often involves a deep fear of failure, stemming from the belief that failure might expose a lack of ability. A growth mindset helps counteract this by reframing how you view failure. Instead of seeing it as a negative reflection of your capabilities, you start to see it as a vital part of the learning process. This reduces the anxiety associated with performance and can decrease the overall intensity of imposter feelings.

People with a growth mindset are more resilient in the face of challenges. They are less likely to feel overwhelmed by the pressure to perform at a consistently high level because they see their growth potential as limitless. This resilience makes it easier to cope with the internal and external pressures that can trigger or exacerbate imposter syndrome.

One of the symptoms of imposter syndrome is the inability to accurately assess one's skills and contributions. A growth mindset encourages a more balanced and honest self-assessment. It allows you to recognize and attribute your accomplishments to your efforts rather than external factors like luck. This can gradually help you internalize your successes and feel more deserving of your role and achievements.

Feedback is crucial for growth and development, but it can be a source of fear for those experiencing imposter syndrome. With a growth mindset, feedback is not a threat but a tool for improvement. This openness to feedback can lead to better performance and increased confidence, further reducing feelings of being an imposter (Delves, 2020).

Tips for Cultivating a Growth Mindset

- **Refresh your routine.** Changing up your daily routine can be a powerful way to stimulate your mind and discover new ways of thinking. Even small changes, like altering your commute or trying a new restaurant, can make a difference.
- **Try one new thing every day.** This practice encourages curiosity and reduces the fear of failure. By consistently stepping out of your comfort zone, you condition yourself to be open to new experiences and learning.
- **Reflect on failures.** End each day by reflecting on what didn't go as planned and what you learned from it. This helps to normalize failure as a part of the learning process rather than something to be avoided.
- **Use the word "yet" more often.** Adding "yet" to statements about your abilities ("I can't do this, yet...") can help reinforce that your current limitations are temporary and surmountable with effort and time.
- **Emphasize growth over speed.** Focus on gradual improvement and learning rather than rushing to achieve quick results. This perspective encourages long-term development instead of short-term gains.
- **Focus on the experience, not the end result.** Enjoy the journey of learning and growth without being overly fixated on the outcomes. This can make the process more enjoyable and less stressful.

- **Be inspired by the success of others**. Instead of feeling threatened by others' achievements, use their stories as motivation. Their successes can show you what's possible with perseverance and effort.
- **Surround yourself with growth-minded people**. Engage with individuals who embrace challenges and are committed to personal development. Their attitudes can influence and reinforce your growth mindset.
- **Celebrate small wins**. Acknowledge and celebrate your progress and the successes of others. This can boost motivation and help build a positive and supportive environment.
- **Cultivate a sense of purpose**. Understanding why you are pursuing your goals can provide motivation and endurance, particularly during challenging times (Davis, 2019; Wooll, 2021).

The strategies discussed earlier in the book, such as challenging self-limiting beliefs and embracing imperfection, can help you overcome imposter syndrome and transition from a fixed to a growth mindset. These approaches dismantle the deep-seated beliefs that can hinder personal and professional growth.

Summary

- **Emphasis on Becoming**: A growth mindset focuses on the continuous process of becoming rather than simply being. It promotes learning, evolving, and transcending previous limits, contrasting with a fixed mindset that views abilities as static. This perspective allows individuals to view challenges and setbacks as opportunities for growth and learning.

- **Impact on Outcomes**: Adopting a growth mindset can profoundly influence personal and professional outcomes. This mindset fosters resilience and encourages individuals to engage with challenges actively, leading to better performance and greater satisfaction. It also helps overcome the fear of failure by reframing setbacks as essential steps in the learning process.
- **Application Across Life's Aspects**: The principles of a growth mindset are applicable not only in academic and professional settings but also in personal relationships and self-improvement. It equips individuals with the resilience to overcome challenges, fosters better relationships through empathy and open communication, and encourages continuous personal growth.
- **Consequences of a Fixed Mindset**: A fixed mindset limits growth by instilling a fear of failure and a reluctance to step outside comfort zones. It often leads to avoiding risks, which stifles both personal and professional development. Understanding and addressing the roots of a fixed mindset can help you shift toward more growth-oriented behaviors.
- **Overcoming Imposter Syndrome**: Imposter syndrome, often tied to a fixed mindset, can be mitigated through the principles of a growth mindset. Viewing failures as learning opportunities and

feedback as a tool for improvement helps build resilience and self-confidence, reducing feelings of being an imposter.

Conclusion

By embracing the concept of "becoming" rather than merely "being," we open ourselves to a world where every challenge is an opportunity for mastery, and every setback teaches resilience. We have learned that a growth mindset transcends individual achievements and influences how we engage with the world. As we conclude this chapter, remember that our abilities are malleable and shaped by our dedication and hard work. This powerful knowledge literally changes how we see the world, ourselves, and our goals.

Looking ahead to Chapter 7, we will delve deeper into the crucial role of self-awareness in transforming our mindset. We will explore practices such as mindfulness, journaling, and seeking feedback, which are vital for cultivating a growth mindset. These tools do more than just enhance our awareness of our thought patterns and behaviors; they empower us to make intentional improvements on our path to personal growth.

Chapter 7
The Power of Self-Awareness

Self-awareness is a skill that impacts various aspects of your life. Dr. Tasha Eurich, an organizational psychologist, best-selling author, and executive coach, emphasizes that self-aware individuals excel in their careers, earn promotions more quickly, and are seen as trusted and effective leaders. Beyond the workplace, they tend to have happier personal relationships and raise well-adjusted children (Talesnik, 2019). Her research highlights the significant advantages of self-awareness in both professional and personal contexts.

Reflect on your level of self-awareness as you begin this chapter. Consider how it affects your interactions at work and your relationships at home. How well do you understand your strengths and weaknesses? How do your thoughts, emotions, and behaviors influence your decisions and actions? Self-awareness is closely related to a growth mindset because it involves recognizing and accepting where you are now while believing in your capacity for growth and improvement.

Embracing this mindset allows you to view feedback and challenges as opportunities to learn and develop rather than threats or failures.

This chapter will help you discover strategies for developing self-awareness and reaping its numerous benefits. We will explore the foundational elements of self-awareness, its impact on various aspects of life, and practical techniques to enhance this vital skill. By the end of this chapter, you will have a deeper understanding of yourself and how to navigate your professional and personal worlds more effectively.

Understanding Self-Awareness

Self-awareness is the foundation of emotional intelligence and a pivotal personal and professional development skill. It's about taking an honest look at yourself—your strengths, weaknesses, thoughts, beliefs, motivations, and emotions—to better understand your unique place in your environment and how you react to it. This helps you guide your actions and respond to people and situations around you in a healthier way. Let's break down the key components contributing to self-awareness and how they influence our interactions and decision-making processes.

Self-discovery plays a crucial role in achieving self-improvement. By engaging in self-awareness, you deeply explore your inner self, gaining a better understanding of your emotions, thoughts, and behaviors. This process of self-discovery helps identify areas for personal growth and improvement. With increased self-knowledge, you can make informed decisions that lead to meaningful life changes.

Embracing self-discovery as a continuous journey fosters ongoing development in both personal and professional aspects of your life.

Emotional Awareness

The journey to emotional intelligence begins with self-awareness. It involves recognizing and understanding your emotions—identifying what you feel, why you feel it, and how these emotions influence your thoughts and actions. This awareness is crucial for managing your emotions effectively, empathizing with others, handling social complexities, and making decisions that lead to positive outcomes. For instance, understanding that you feel overwhelmed by planning a family event allows you to take proactive steps, such as delegating tasks or seeking help, rather than letting the stress negatively affect your mood and the event.

Understanding Thought Patterns

Self-awareness also means being aware of your thought processes. Our thoughts can be optimistic, pessimistic, rational, or irrational, and they significantly affect our emotions and behavior. By identifying and understanding these patterns, you can challenge detrimental thoughts and reinforce positive ones, thereby enhancing your decision-making and overall well-being. For example, if you catch yourself thinking, "I always mess things up," during a project review, recognizing this pattern enables you to counter it with reminders of past successes and focus on constructive feedback, fostering a growth mindset.

Recognizing Actions and Reactions

Self-awareness extends to understanding how your actions and reactions affect those around you. Simple acknowledgments, like how your tone of voice can defuse or escalate a situation, are part of this awareness. By observing your behaviors and their impacts, you can make conscious choices to modify your actions, improving your relationships and interactions. For instance, if raising your voice during your children's homework time leads to upset and resistance, recognizing this helps you adopt a more patient and supportive demeanor.

Impact on Self and Others

A critical aspect of self-awareness is appreciating how your behaviors and emotions influence yourself and others. Knowing that your openness makes people feel welcomed can encourage stronger and more positive relationships in personal and professional settings.

Impact of Self-Awareness

Self-awareness can profoundly impact your personal growth and well-being by enhancing your decision-making abilities, improving your relationships, and promoting overall happiness. When you develop self-awareness, you gain a deeper understanding of your emotional and physical needs, leading you to make healthier life choices.

Awareness invites change. When you become aware of your thoughts, emotions, and behaviors, you create an opportunity for transformation. Awareness acts as a catalyst for change, enabling you to recognize patterns that no longer serve you and adopt new, healthier ones. By consciously acknowledging your current state, you empower yourself to take proactive steps toward positive change. This awareness facilitates better physical and mental health as you make informed decisions that align with your well-being, such as getting adequate rest and managing stress effectively (Dempsey, 2023).

In terms of relationships, as a self-aware individual, you communicate more effectively because you understand your own emotions and reactions better. This leads to stronger, more meaningful connections with others, as you can express your needs clearly and empathize with the feelings of others (Soken-Huberty, 2023). Moreover, self-awareness enhances decision-making by providing insights into your thoughts and emotional triggers. You become capable of making decisions that reflect your long-term goals rather than reacting impulsively to immediate circumstances.

Furthermore, self-awareness is crucial for achieving success in both your personal and professional life. It allows you to align your actions with your values and objectives, recognize your strengths and weaknesses, and seize growth opportunities. Real-life examples of the benefits of self-awareness include individuals like you who have changed career paths for more fulfilling roles or improved their interpersonal relationships by adjusting their behaviors and emotional responses accordingly.

For instance, consider someone who has spent years in a well-paying but unsatisfying job. Through increased self-awareness, they realize their true passion lies in a completely different field. This insight motivates them to make a bold career change, leading to a role that fulfills them and aligns with their deeper values and life goals. This transition exemplifies how self-awareness can guide individuals to make significant life changes that enhance their personal satisfaction and professional success.

Similarly, in relationships, self-awareness is pivotal in fostering deeper connections and understanding. Imagine someone who frequently finds themselves in arguments with their partner over seemingly trivial matters. Through self-reflection, they understand that these reactions stem from deeper insecurities rather than surface issues. Armed with this insight, they begin to address their insecurities and communicate more openly about their feelings rather than lashing out. This change improves their relationship dynamics and strengthens their emotional bond with their partner, showing how self-awareness can transform personal interactions and lead to more harmonious and supportive relationships.

The Synergistic Relationship between Self-Awareness and Growth Mindset

Self-awareness and a growth mindset are deeply interconnected, each enhancing the effectiveness of the other in a continuous cycle of personal development. When you cultivate self-awareness, you gain a clear understanding of your current abilities, emotional responses, and the underlying motivations behind your actions. This knowledge is crucial because it sets the stage for a growth mindset, wherein you acknowledge your current state but recognize the potential for improvement and growth (*How Does Mindset Impact Self-Awareness?* n.d.).

Conversely, adopting a growth mindset enhances self-awareness by encouraging the pursuit of self-reflection and openness to feedback. For instance, as you embrace challenges and reflect on various outcomes, whether successes or setbacks, you develop a deeper understanding of how you respond to different situations, which in turn increases your emotional and cognitive self-awareness. This self-awareness feeds back into strengthening your growth mindset by highlighting areas where growth is necessary and possible.

This reciprocal relationship can be seen in everyday scenarios, such as learning a new skill or adapting to change. Suppose you begin learning a musical instrument. A growth mindset prompts you to view each practice session as an opportunity to improve rather than a test of your unchangeable musical talent. When you notice improvements or areas needing more work, your self-awareness grows, providing valuable insights into how you learn best, what strategies are effective, and how emotions like frustration or excitement affect your performance. This awareness then encourages you to adjust your approach, further fostering a growth mindset that is open to continuous learning and adaptation (Ballesteros, 2018).

Mindfulness

Mindfulness is a state of active, open attention to the present, where you observe your thoughts, feelings, and sensations without judgment. This practice, rooted in Buddhist and Hindu teachings, has gained significant attention in the Western world, primarily through the work of Jon Kabat-Zinn, who developed the Mindfulness-Based Stress Reduction (MBSR) program in the late 1970s. Let's explore what mindfulness is, its benefits, and how you can incorporate it into your daily life.

What Is Mindfulness?

Mindfulness involves being fully present and engaged in the current moment, aware of your thoughts, emotions, and sensations without trying to change them. It is about reawakening oneself to the present rather than dwelling on the past or anticipating the future. This practice can help you develop a non-judgmental awareness and acceptance of your experiences (*Mindfulness*, n.d.).

Benefits of Practicing Mindfulness

- **Enhanced Self-Awareness:** Mindfulness helps you become more aware of your internal states and surroundings, allowing you to observe your thoughts and emotions without reacting to them. This increased self-awareness can prevent automatic, destructive habits and promote healthier responses to various situations.

- **Emotional Regulation**: By practicing mindfulness, you can learn to manage difficult emotions more effectively. This practice allows you to observe your feelings without judgment, creating space between you and your emotional reactions. This space enables you to respond more calmly and thoughtfully to challenging situations.
- **Reduced Stress and Anxiety**: Mindfulness has been shown to lower stress levels and reduce symptoms of anxiety and depression. Focusing on the present moment and accepting your thoughts and feelings can alleviate the mental burden of worrying about the past or future.
- **Improved Cognitive Function**: Regular mindfulness practice can enhance cognitive abilities, including attention, memory, and problem-solving skills. It can also slow brain aging and improve overall brain health.
- **Better Quality of Life**: Mindfulness can improve your overall well-being, help manage pain, and enhance the quality of life for those with chronic conditions. It promotes a sense of peace and contentment by fostering a deeper connection to the present moment (Hoshaw, 2022).

Exercises

Body Scan Meditation

A body scan meditation is a simple yet powerful mindfulness practice that involves paying close attention to sensations in different parts of the body. Regular practice can enhance self-awareness, reduce stress, and promote a sense of calm and well-being. By dedicating a small part of your day to this practice, you can significantly improve your connection to your body and mind. Here's how to do it (Raypole, 2020; Richardson, 2022):

1. Get comfortable.

- Find a quiet place where you won't be disturbed.
- Sit in a comfortable chair or lie down on your back. Make sure your body is supported.

2. Close your eyes.

- Gently close your eyes to eliminate visual distractions and help you focus inward.

3. Focus on your breath.

- Take a few deep breaths, noticing the sensation of air entering and leaving your body.
- Allow your breath to return to its natural rhythm.

4. Begin the scan.

- Start at one end of your body—either your head or your toes.
- Bring your attention to this area and notice any sensations. This might include warmth, tingling, pressure, or even the absence of any sensation.

5. Move slowly and methodically.

- Gradually move your attention to the next part of your body. If you start at your toes, move up to your feet, then ankles, calves, and so on.
- Spend a few moments on each body part before moving on.

6. Observe without judgment.

- Simply observe the sensations as they are without trying to change anything.
- If your mind wanders, gently bring your focus back to the part of the body you were observing.

7. Acknowledge discomfort.

- If you encounter areas of tension, pain, or discomfort, acknowledge these sensations without judgment. Breathe into these areas and imagine the tension melting away with each exhale.

8. Continue until you've scanned your whole body.

- Continue the scan methodically until you've reached the other end of your body.

9. Bring your awareness back.

- Once you have completed the scan, take a few deep breaths.

- Gently bring your awareness back to your surroundings.
- Open your eyes slowly and take a moment to notice how you feel.

Mindful Breathing

Mindful breathing can improve your well-being by reducing stress, promoting relaxation, and enhancing mental clarity. By focusing on your breath, you can stay present and calm. Here are three techniques to help you get started: Breath awareness meditation, deep breathing, and the 4-7-8 breathing technique. Each method offers unique benefits and can be easily added to your daily routine.

Breath Awareness Meditation

Breath awareness meditation is a simple practice that involves observing the natural rhythm of your breath without trying to control it. Here's how to do it (Fargo, 2016):

1. Find a comfortable position. Sit or lie down in a quiet place.
2. Close your eyes. This helps reduce distractions.
3. Focus on your breath. Notice the sensation of air entering your nose. Feel the rise and fall of your belly, and pay attention to the rhythm of your breathing.
4. Observe without judgment. Simply watch your breath as it flows naturally. If your mind wanders, gently bring your attention back to your breath.

Deep Breathing

Deep breathing can help reduce stress and improve relaxation. Follow these steps to practice deep breathing (*Deep Breathing Exercise*, 2016):

1. Get comfortable. Sit or lie down, and loosen any tight clothing.
2. Place your hands. Put one hand on your chest and the other on your belly.
3. Breathe in. Take a slow, deep breath through your nose, filling your belly with air (your belly should rise more than your chest).
4. Breathe out. Exhale slowly through your mouth.
5. Repeat. Continue this pattern, aiming for a rhythm of four seconds in and four seconds out.

4-7-8 Breathing Technique

The 4-7-8 breathing technique promotes relaxation and reduces anxiety (Fletcher, 2019).

1. Get comfortable. Sit or lie down in a comfortable position.
2. Place the tip of your tongue. Touch the tip of your tongue to the ridge of tissue just behind your upper front teeth.
3. Exhale completely. Let all the air out through your mouth, making a whooshing sound.
4. Inhale quietly. Breathe in through your nose for a count of four.

5. **Hold your breath.** Hold your breath for a count of seven.
6. **Exhale forcefully.** Exhale completely through your mouth, making a whooshing sound for a count of eight.
7. **Repeat.** Complete the cycle up to four times.

Mindfulness Meditation

Mindfulness meditation involves focusing on your breath and bringing your mind back when it wanders. Here's how to practice it (Cherry, 2021; *How to Practice Mindfulness Meditation*, 2018):

1. **Take your seat.** Sit in a stable, comfortable position on a chair or cushion.
2. **Notice your legs.** If you're on a cushion, cross your legs. If you're on a chair, rest your feet flat on the floor.
3. **Straighten your upper body.** Keep your back straight but not stiff.
4. **Relax your arms.** Place your hands on your legs with your upper arms parallel to your torso.
5. **Lower your gaze.** Drop your chin slightly and let your gaze fall gently downward, or close your eyes if you prefer.
6. **Focus on your breath.** Pay attention to the sensation of your breath as it goes in and out. Notice the air moving through your nose or mouth and the rise and fall of your belly.

7. **Acknowledge wandering thoughts.** When your mind wanders, gently bring your focus back to your breath without judgment.
8. **Stay for a while.** Continue this practice for a set amount of time, starting with a few minutes and gradually increasing.

Incorporating Mindfulness into Daily Life

Mindfulness can be seamlessly integrated into your daily routines. Here are practical tips and techniques to help you incorporate mindfulness into your everyday life:

Observe Your Surroundings

Take moments throughout your day to pause and observe your environment. This practice helps ground you in the present moment and increases your awareness of the world around you. For instance, when you're outside, notice the colors of the leaves, the sounds of birds, or the feel of the wind on your skin. These small observations can enhance your sense of presence and mindfulness (Scott, 2019).

Practice Mindful Eating

Mindful eating involves giving your full attention to the experience of eating and drinking. Notice the colors, textures, and smells of your food. Pay attention to the flavors and how they change as you chew. This practice enhances your enjoyment of food and helps you become more aware of your body's hunger and fullness cues, reducing overeating and promoting healthier eating habits (Tallon, 2020).

Be Mindful in Your Interactions

Mindfulness in interactions means giving your full attention to the person you are with, whether it's a colleague, friend, or family member. Listen actively without planning your response while they are speaking. Observe their body language and tone of voice. This practice can improve your relationships by fostering deeper connections and reducing misunderstandings.

Check-In with Your Body

Regularly take moments to scan your body and notice any areas of tension or discomfort. You can do this while sitting at your desk, standing in line, or lying in bed. Bring your attention to different body parts, from your head to your toes, and notice how each part feels. This practice helps you stay connected to your body and can provide insights into your physical and emotional state (*5 Ways to Get Mindfulness into Your Everyday Life*, n.d.).

Pause throughout the Day

Set aside moments throughout your day to pause and just be. These pauses can be as short as a few breaths or as long as a few minutes. Use these moments to check in with your breath, body, and mind. This practice can help reset your focus, reduce stress, and increase your overall well-being.

Engage in Activities Mindfully

Whatever activity you are engaged in, do it with full attention. Whether you're washing the dishes, walking the dog, or typing an email, bring your awareness to the task at hand. Notice the sensations, movements, and sounds involved. This practice can turn even mundane tasks into opportunities for mindfulness and presence (*7 Easy Ways to Be Mindful in Your Everyday Life*, n.d.).

Journaling

As we begin this new section on journaling, it's worth noting that we've talked about journaling a few times in this book. We've highlighted how journaling helps you process emotions and thoughts, bringing clarity and reducing stress. It also supports a growth mindset by encouraging you to reflect on your goals, progress, and setbacks, aiding in personal development. Additionally, journaling is a great tool for healing emotional wounds and understanding your patterns and behaviors (McD, 2020). Now, let's dive deeper into how journaling can enhance mindfulness and help positively shift your mindset.

Journaling provides a dedicated space to reflect on your thoughts, emotions, and experiences, leading to greater self-awareness (Tartakovsky, 2022). By putting your thoughts into words, you can better understand your internal world and how it influences your actions and decisions. This practice helps you identify patterns and triggers and fosters a deeper connection with yourself (Walichowski, 2018).

Consider someone who regularly journals about their daily experiences. Over time, they may notice a recurring theme of stress related to work deadlines. By recognizing this pattern, they can take proactive steps to manage their workload more effectively, such as setting realistic goals or seeking support from colleagues. This insight into their stressors and the subsequent actions taken to address them can significantly improve their overall well-being and productivity.

Getting Started

Here are some practical tips to help you begin if you haven't already:

- **Take a micro-step.** Start small to avoid feeling overwhelmed. Set a timer for just one or two minutes a day for your journaling session.
- **Find the journaling techniques that work for you.** Experiment with different methods, such as writing in a notebook, using a digital app, or even voice recording. Choose what feels most comfortable and sustainable for you.
- **Schedule your journaling into your day.** Dedicate a specific time each day for journaling. It could be in the morning to set intentions for the day or in the evening to reflect on your experiences.
- **Pick the simplest tools.** Use a plain notebook and a pen. The simpler, the better, to minimize distractions and make the practice feel more accessible.

- **Get creative**. Feel free to draw, doodle, or use colors to express your thoughts and emotions. Creativity can make journaling more engaging and enjoyable.
- **Let it all out**. Write freely without censoring yourself. Let your thoughts flow naturally, and don't worry about grammar or spelling.
- **Try free writing**. Set a timer and write continuously for a set period without stopping. This technique helps bypass the inner critic and uncovers deeper thoughts and feelings.
- **Explore a prompt**. Use journal prompts to guide your writing. Prompts can provide a starting point and stimulate reflection on specific topics.
- **Analyze what isn't working**. Reflect on aspects of your life that aren't going well. Consider why they are problematic and explore possible solutions through your writing.
- **Keep a journal handy in your bag**. Carry your journal with you to jot down thoughts and observations throughout the day. This helps capture insights in real-time and makes journaling a continuous process.

Prompts for Self-Awareness and Self-Discovery

Use the blank pages at the end of this book or whatever else you have at hand to explore these ten journal prompts designed to enhance self-awareness and foster self-discovery. Remember, the key to effective journaling is consistency and openness. Allow yourself the freedom to express and explore without judgment, and you will discover the profound benefits of this practice.

1. What personal values are most important to me? How do my daily actions reflect these values?
2. Describe a recent situation where you faced a challenge. What strategies did you use to overcome it, and what did you learn about yourself in the process?
3. List three things you appreciate about your life right now. Why are they important to you?
4. Think about a significant event in your life. How did it shape your current beliefs and behaviors?
5. What recurring thoughts and emotions have you noticed recently? What messages might they be conveying?
6. Identify your key strengths. How can you leverage them more effectively in your everyday life?
7. Recall a moment when you felt completely at peace. What elements contributed to this feeling?
8. Outline your short-term and long-term goals. How do these goals align with your passions and values?
9. How do you usually respond to criticism or feedback? What insights can you gain from your typical reactions?
10. Reflect on an area of your life where you feel stagnant. What steps can you take to move forward and create positive change?

Seeking Feedback

Feedback is a powerful tool for personal and professional growth. It involves receiving information or criticism about prior actions or behaviors, which can be used to adjust and improve future actions and behaviors (DeFranzo, 2018). There are several types of feedback: informal feedback, which consists of spontaneous and casual comments; formal feedback, which is structured and planned, such as annual performance reviews; constructive feedback, which provides specific and actionable observations aimed at improvement; analytical feedback, which is data-driven and often used in performance metrics; and motivational feedback, which includes encouraging comments that boost morale and motivation (*10 Feedback Styles*, 2022).

Embracing feedback with a growth mindset allows you to see critiques not as personal attacks but as valuable information for guiding your personal and professional growth. When you receive feedback, you gain insights into areas you might not have noticed on your own, helping you identify strengths and areas for development. This perspective encourages continuous learning and improvement, reinforcing the belief that abilities can be developed through effort and practice.

Practical Guidance for Seeking Feedback Effectively

Seeking feedback effectively is essential for personal growth in professional and personal relationships. To make the most of the feedback process, it is important to approach it strategically and thoughtfully.

Reflect on What You Hope to Gain

Before seeking feedback, take a moment to reflect on what you hope to learn. Are you looking for insights into your performance at work, how you interact with colleagues, or how you relate to friends and family? Clarifying your goals helps you effectively frame your feedback request, ensuring you receive relevant and actionable insights. By understanding what you want to gain from the feedback, you can approach the process with a clear focus and purpose.

Identify the Right People to Ask for Feedback

Choosing the right individuals to ask for feedback is crucial. Select people familiar with your work and personal life and whose opinions you trust. These could be colleagues, mentors, supervisors, friends, or family members who can provide honest and constructive feedback. Their familiarity with different aspects of your life ensures that the feedback you receive is informed and relevant, making it more valuable for your growth and development.

Prepare the Right Questions

Formulating specific questions is key to getting targeted and useful feedback. Think about the areas you want to focus on and prepare questions that address those topics. For example, you might ask a colleague, "Can you provide feedback on my recent presentation?" or a friend, "How do you feel about our communication lately?" Specific questions help guide the feedback process, making it easier for the feedback provider to give detailed and actionable insights.

Take Notes on Your Feedback

When receiving feedback, it is important to document the information you receive. Take notes to ensure you remember the details and can refer back to them later. This practice helps track your progress and identify patterns over time. By keeping a record of the feedback, you can review it periodically to assess your growth and make adjustments as needed.

Listen and Be Willing to Accept Information with a Positive, Open Mind

Approach feedback with an open mind and a positive attitude. Focus on understanding the information rather than defending yourself. This attitude fosters a constructive dialogue and enhances learning. By being receptive to feedback, you can gain valuable insights to help you improve and grow.

Ask Clarifying Questions

If you do not fully understand the feedback, ask for clarification. Questions like "Can you give me an example of what you mean?" can provide deeper insights and ensure you correctly interpret the feedback. Clarifying questions helps you gain a clearer understanding of the feedback, making it easier to apply the suggestions effectively.

Use the Feedback to Help You Improve, Not to Beat Yourself Up

The purpose of feedback is to facilitate improvement, not self-criticism. Focus on actionable steps you can take to enhance your performance and skills. Instead of dwelling on any negative aspects of the feedback, use it as a guide to identify areas for growth and development.

Commit and Follow Up

Show commitment to improvement by setting specific goals based on the feedback and following up on them. Checking in with your feedback providers periodically can help track your progress and keep you accountable. Follow-up conversations also allow you to seek additional guidance and support as you work toward your goals (Mether, 2018; *Receiving and Giving Effective Feedback*, 2019; Weller, 2019).

Giving Effective Feedback to Promote Self-Awareness in Others

Giving effective feedback can help others develop self-awareness and a growth mindset, leading to significant personal and professional growth. When used correctly, feedback is a powerful tool for improvement.

Get Clear on the Purpose of the Feedback

Be clear about why you are giving feedback. Whether it is to acknowledge good work, suggest improvements, or evaluate performance, having clarity helps you deliver effective feedback. For instance, if you're providing feedback to a colleague, explain that your goal is to help them improve their project management skills. In personal relationships, clarify that your feedback is meant to enhance communication or resolve conflicts.

Be Conscious of Timing

Choose an appropriate time to provide feedback. Delivering feedback promptly after an event ensures it is relevant and actionable. For example, give feedback soon after a meeting or a completed task in a professional setting. In personal situations, address issues soon after they occur to keep the feedback timely and effective. This approach ensures the feedback is fresh in both your minds and can be acted upon immediately.

Ask How the Person Would Like to Receive Feedback

Respect individual preferences for receiving feedback. Some people may prefer face-to-face discussions, while others might like written feedback. Ask the person their preferred method to ensure the feedback is received in the most comfortable and effective way. Some might prefer a formal meeting in a work context, while others might appreciate a quick email. Consider whether a face-to-face talk or a written message would be more appropriate in personal relationships.

Be Specific

Provide clear and specific feedback by highlighting particular behaviors or actions. Specificity helps the recipient understand exactly what needs to be improved or continued. For instance, instead of saying, "You need to communicate better," say, "I noticed that you often interrupt others during meetings. Letting them finish might improve our discussions." This clarity helps the person know exactly what behavior to address.

Concentrate on the Behavior, Not the Person

Focus on specific behaviors rather than making personal judgments. This approach ensures the feedback is constructive and not perceived as a personal attack. For example, instead of saying, "You are always late," say, "I've noticed you've been arriving late to our last few meetings. Can we discuss what's causing this?" This way, the feedback is about the behavior and not an attack on the person.

Make It Actionable (And Future-Focused When Possible)

Provide actionable suggestions that the recipient can implement. Focus on future improvements rather than just past mistakes. For instance, if you are giving feedback on a project, suggest specific steps they can take to improve their work. In personal situations, offer concrete ways to improve interactions, such as setting aside time each week to discuss any issues (Centre for Teaching Excellence, 2019).

Offer Continuing Support

Follow up with the person to offer support and check on their progress. Continuous feedback and support help sustain improvement and development. In a professional setting, this could mean regular check-ins to discuss progress. Personal relationships might involve ongoing conversations to ensure issues are resolved and improvements are made (McLeod, 2015).

Summary

- **Recognizing the Importance of Self-Awareness**: Understand that self-awareness is crucial for your professional success and personal well-being. By becoming more self-aware, you can excel in your career, earn promotions faster, and enjoy more satisfying personal relationships. Reflect on your level of self-awareness and consider how it impacts various aspects of your life.

- **Understanding the Components of Self-Awareness**: Realize that self-awareness involves understanding your emotions, thought patterns, and behaviors. By recognizing and understanding these elements, you can manage your emotions better, make informed decisions, and improve your interactions with others. Pay attention to these components and their influence on your actions and decisions.
- **Improved Relationships and Decision-Making**: Developing self-awareness can lead to stronger relationships and better decision-making. By understanding your emotions and reactions, you can communicate more effectively and build deeper connections with others. Additionally, enhanced self-awareness allows you to make decisions that align with your long-term goals rather than reacting impulsively.
- **Adopting a Growth Mindset**: Embrace the connection between self-awareness and a growth mindset. Recognize your current state and believe in your capacity for improvement. By adopting a growth mindset, you can enhance your self-awareness and vice versa, creating a continuous cycle of personal growth.
- **Using Practical Techniques to Enhance Self-Awareness**: Apply practical strategies for developing self-awareness, such as mindfulness practices, journaling, and seeking feedback. These techniques

will help you gain a deeper understanding of yourself and improve your ability to navigate both professional and personal challenges effectively.

Conclusion

In this chapter, we explored self-awareness and its impact on our personal and professional lives. We looked at the key components of self-awareness, such as emotional awareness, thought patterns, and recognizing actions and reactions. Understanding these elements can improve our emotional intelligence, relationships, and decision-making.

Remember, self-awareness is linked to a growth mindset. By embracing self-awareness, you acknowledge your current state while believing in your potential for growth. This mindset helps you see feedback and challenges as opportunities to learn and improve.

The next chapter will focus on strategies to maintain a positive and growth-oriented mindset. We will discuss the importance of self-care, building a supportive network, setting personal goals, tracking progress, and celebrating success. These strategies will help you handle life's challenges and promote personal and professional growth.

Stay curious and engaged as we continue this journey. Developing self-awareness and a growth mindset will open new paths to success. Let's move forward with the tools and insights we've gained, ready to embrace the next steps toward personal growth and fulfillment.

Part 4
Sustaining Positive Changes

Chapter 8
Additional Strategies for Lasting Success

 "The biggest thing holding you back is almost always... you. Start there."

— Hunter Post

In our journey to overcome self-imposed limitations, we have explored how self-limiting beliefs, negative thinking, fears, and self-sabotage behaviors act as barriers to success. Recognizing these obstacles is the crucial first step toward overcoming them. We have discussed strategies such as cultivating a growth mindset and increasing self-awareness as foundational approaches to breaking through these barriers.

However, there are additional complementary methods to consider. One of the most vital of these is engaging in self-care. Taking ownership of your actions and choices through self-care practices is essential for driving meaningful change in your life. Self-care extends beyond indulgence it involves nurturing your physical, emotional, mental, social, professional, financial, and spiritual well-being.

This chapter will explore practical self-care activities and demonstrate how integrating these into your routine can help manage stress, build resilience, and maintain a positive outlook. By prioritizing self-care, you empower yourself to enhance creativity, improve problem-solving skills, and support overall personal growth and development. You will be better equipped to take control of your life and make significant, positive changes.

Engaging in Self-Care

The narrative around self-care often revolves around indulgent activities like spa days or treating oneself to luxury items. However, self-care is much broader and deeper than these misconceptions suggest. It encompasses a variety of activities, from getting enough sleep and eating healthy foods to enjoying a spa day or a relaxing walk. Self-care helps you manage stress, build resilience, and stay positive. By taking care of yourself, you can boost your creativity, problem-solving skills, and overall well-being, which supports personal growth and development. For example, regular exercise can increase your energy and improve mental clarity, while meditation can reduce stress and help you focus better.

Types of Self-Care

Have you ever considered all the different ways you can care for yourself? Self-care isn't just about one aspect of your life; it spans physical, emotional, mental, social, professional, financial, and spiritual well-being. Let's explore various types of self-care and how you can incorporate them into your routine.

Physical Self-Care

- **Exercise regularly.** Incorporate activities like walking, jogging, yoga, or dancing.
- **Eat balanced meals.** Include fruits, vegetables, lean proteins, and whole grains.
- **Get enough sleep.** Aim for seven to nine hours each night.
- **Stay hydrated.** Drink plenty of water.
- **Maintain good hygiene.** Regularly bathe, brush your teeth, and keep clean.

Emotional Self-Care

- **Journal your feelings.** Write down your thoughts and emotions.
- **Practice mindfulness.** Engage in meditation or deep-breathing exercises.
- **Seek therapy.** Talk to a mental health professional if needed.
- **Spend time on hobbies.** Do activities that bring you joy.

- **Set boundaries.** Learn to say no and protect your emotional energy.

Mental Self-Care

- **Read books.** Enjoy novels, self-help books, or educational material.
- **Learn something new.** Take up a new hobby or online course.
- **Solve puzzles.** Keep your mind sharp with crosswords or brainteasers.
- **Practice positive affirmations.** Encourage yourself with daily positive statements.
- **Limit screen time.** Take breaks from screens to rest your eyes and mind.

Social Self-Care

- **Connect with loved ones.** Spend time with family and friends.
- **Join a club or group.** Participate in community activities or interest groups.
- **Volunteer.** Offer your time and skills to help others.
- **Plan social activities.** Organize outings or virtual meet-ups.
- **Communicate openly.** Share your feelings and listen to others.

Professional Self-Care

- **Take breaks.** Step away from work regularly to recharge.
- **Set realistic goals.** Break tasks into manageable steps.
- **Maintain work-life balance.** Separate work from personal life.
- **Seek mentorship.** Find a mentor to guide you.
- **Continue learning.** Attend workshops and training sessions to enhance your skills.

Financial Self-Care

- **Create a budget.** Plan your expenses and stick to it.
- **Save regularly.** Set aside a portion of your income.
- **Invest wisely.** Consider long-term investment options.
- **Avoid unnecessary debt.** Spend within your means.
- **Seek financial advice.** Consult a financial advisor for guidance.

Spiritual Self-Care

- **Meditate or pray.** Spend time in quiet reflection or prayer.
- **Spend time in nature.** Connect with the outdoors.
- **Attend religious services.** Participate in spiritual gatherings.
- **Read inspirational texts.** Engage with spiritual or philosophical readings.

- **Practice gratitude.** Keep a gratitude journal and reflect on your blessings.

Practical Tips for Incorporating Self-Care

In our busy lives, finding time for self-care can be challenging. However, making the most of your limited time can significantly improve your well-being. Here are some practical tips to help you incorporate self-care into your daily routine, even when time is tight:

Start Small

Begin with simple activities that are easy to fit into your daily life. For example, take a five-minute walk, enjoy a cup of tea, or spend a few minutes practicing deep breathing.

Schedule Time for Self-Care

Make self-care a priority by scheduling it into your daily routine. Set aside specific times each day or week for activities that nourish your mind, body, and soul.

Create Reminders

Use alarms, sticky notes, or apps to remind you to take breaks and practice self-care. These prompts can help you stay consistent, especially when you're busy.

Designate a Space for Self-Care

Create a dedicated space for self-care, whether it's a cozy corner for reading, a mat for yoga, or a comfortable chair for meditation. Having a specific area can make it easier to focus and relax.

Focus on Consistency

Consistency is key. Even small, regular activities can have a big impact over time. Aim to include self-care in your daily routine, no matter how busy you are.

Do What You Enjoy

Choose activities that you genuinely enjoy. Whether gardening, painting, or listening to music, doing things you love makes self-care feel like a treat, not a chore.

Be Present

When practicing self-care, focus on the moment. Avoid multitasking and fully engage in the activity. This mindfulness can enhance the relaxing and rejuvenating effects of self-care.

Find an Accountability Buddy

Share your self-care goals with a friend or family member who can help keep you accountable. Check in with each other regularly to share progress, encourage one another, and stay motivated (McEvoy, 2023).

Making Course Corrections and Embracing Change

While practicing self-care and setting goals, it's important to remember that life can be unpredictable. Sometimes, you may find yourself off track or facing unexpected challenges. When this happens, it's crucial to make a course correction—adjust your actions and plans to get back on track. Imagine flying a plane: if you veer off course, you must correct your path to reach your destination.

One change often leads to another, creating a domino effect. Making a positive change in your life can lead to other good changes. For example, starting a regular exercise routine might inspire you to eat healthier, which could improve your sleep and overall well-being.

Finally, don't miss the connecting flight. Each step in your journey to success is interconnected, like catching connecting flights to reach your final destination. Stay on track with your plans and make timely adjustments to avoid missing key opportunities for growth and improvement.

Self-Care Strategies Highlighted in the Book

You may now recognize that many other strategies mentioned throughout this book can also be considered forms of self-care. These techniques help maintain mental and emotional well-being, foster personal growth, and support overall health.

- **Reflective Prompts**: Encouraging introspection and self-awareness
- **Positive Self-Talk**: Promoting a healthier mindset through encouraging inner dialogue
- **Cognitive Restructuring**: Changing unhelpful thought patterns
- **Thought Records**: Identifying and adjusting responses to stress
- **Self-Compassion**: Treating oneself with kindness and understanding

- **Mindfulness**: Staying present and reducing anxiety
- **Asking for and Providing Constructive Feedback**: Enhancing personal and professional growth
- **Building a Supportive Network**: Creating a community for support and encouragement
- **Setting SMART Goals**: Achieving clear, attainable objectives

Surrounding Yourself with Support

A support system is a network of people who provide emotional, mental, and practical assistance when you need it most. This network can include family, friends, coworkers, mentors, and online communities. Research shows that those with robust social support networks tend to have better health, longer lives, and higher levels of well-being. Supportive relationships can help you cope with stress, provide practical help, and offer a sense of belonging and security (*Developing Your Support System*, n.d.; Harper, n.d.).

Benefits of a Support System

A strong support system offers numerous benefits:

- **Reduces Stress**: Sharing your problems with supportive people helps to alleviate stress and anxiety.
- **Improves Self-Esteem**: Knowing others believe in you boosts your confidence and self-worth.

- **Enhances Resilience**: Supportive relationships can make you more resilient in the face of challenges and setbacks.
- **Promotes Better Health**: Good social support is linked to better physical and mental health outcomes (Ashbridge, 2023; Cherry, 2023b).

Tips for Identifying and Building a Supportive Network

By surrounding yourself with supportive people who share and reinforce a growth mindset, you create an environment conducive to personal development and emotional well-being.

- **Meet neighbors and coworkers**. Engage with the people you see regularly. Building relationships with neighbors and coworkers can create a strong local support network.
- **Join professional organizations**. Becoming a member of professional groups can expand your network and connect you with like-minded individuals.
- **Attend workshops**. Participate in workshops and seminars related to your interests or career. These events are great for meeting people who share your goals and aspirations.
- **Volunteer**. Volunteering for causes you care about can introduce you to others with similar values and interests.
- **Take up a sport or join a gym**. Physical activities improve your health and offer opportunities to make new friends.

- **Participate in online communities.** Online groups and forums can provide support and connection, especially if you have niche interests or limited local options.
- **Find support systems in faith-based communities.** Religious and spiritual groups can offer a strong sense of community and support.
- **Build bonds with existing family and friends.** Strengthen your current relationships by spending quality time together and communicating openly (*Build a Support System, 2020*).

Tips for Nurturing Your Support System

Building and nurturing a strong support system is a continuous process that enhances your quality of life.

- **Know what you want from a support system.** Be clear about your needs and expectations. This helps you seek out the right kind of support.
- **Keep the lines of communication open.** Regular, honest communication is essential for maintaining strong relationships.
- **Accept their help.** Don't hesitate to accept support when it's offered. It keeps the relationship balanced and shows you value their assistance.
- **Be available when you're needed.** Reciprocity is key. Make sure you are there for your supporters when they need help.
- **Show appreciation.** Regularly express gratitude to those in your support network.

- **Be a good listener.** Listening is just as important as sharing. Be attentive and supportive when others confide in you.
- **Remember that it's okay to be vulnerable.** Allow yourself to show vulnerability. It can strengthen your bonds and make the support more meaningful.
- **Support successes.** Celebrate the achievements of those in your support system. It reinforces positive relationships.
- **Respect needs and limits.** Understand and respect the personal boundaries of those in your network.
- **Know when a relationship isn't working for you.** If a relationship becomes draining or toxic, it might be best to distance yourself or end it. Prioritize your well-being.

Setting Personal Goals

Goals and mindset are intimately connected, influencing each other in powerful ways. A positive mindset shapes our goals, making them more achievable and meaningful. When we set goals, they can enhance our mindset by providing direction, motivation, and a sense of purpose. Approaching goals with a growth mindset can maximize their power (Dweck, 2006).

Examples of Goals

Goals can be set in multiple areas of life, each contributing to our overall well-being and fulfillment:

- **Career Advancement**: Aiming for a promotion, acquiring a new certification, or expanding professional networks.
- **Skill Acquisition**: Learning a new language, mastering a musical instrument, or developing coding skills.
- **Health and Wellness**: Setting fitness goals, adopting a healthier diet, or committing to a regular meditation practice.
- **Personal Relationships**: Improving communication with a partner, spending quality time with family, or building new friendships (Ravelo, 2021).

Importance of Setting Goals Aligned with Core Values

Setting goals that resonate with one's core values and aspirations ensures they are meaningful and sustainable. Goals aligned with personal values are more likely to be achieved and bring satisfaction. Reflect on your values, passions, and long-term vision to set goals that truly matter to you. By understanding and aligning your goals with your values, you create a roadmap that is achievable and deeply rewarding (Jewell, n.d.). Here are some reflective prompts to help align your goals with your core values:

- What activities or achievements make you feel fulfilled?
- What are the most important principles that guide your life?
- How do you want to impact the world around you?

Introducing the SMART Criteria

The SMART criteria is a widely recognized method for setting effective goals. By setting SMART goals, you can systematically work toward achieving your personal and professional aspirations, ensuring that each step you take is purposeful and aligned with your overall vision. SMART stands for Specific, Measurable, Achievable, Relevant, and Time-bound:

- **Specific**: Clearly define the goal. Instead of "Get fit," specify "Run three times a week."
- **Measurable**: Establish criteria for measuring progress. For example, "Lose 10 pounds in three months."
- **Achievable**: Set realistic goals. "Run a 5k marathon in six months" is more attainable than "Run a marathon next month."
- **Relevant**: Ensure the goal is relevant to your life and values. If career advancement is important, a goal might be "Complete a professional development course."
- **Time-Bound**: Set a deadline to create urgency. "Learn Spanish within a year" sets a clear timeframe (*Goal Setting for Success*, 2024).

Here's an example of a SMART goal for personal development: "Read one book on personal development each month for the next six months." Breaking down larger goals into actionable steps is crucial. For example, if your goal is to write a book, start with steps like "outline the first three chapters this month" or "write 500 words daily."

Tracking Progress and Celebrating Success

Tracking progress and celebrating milestones are crucial for achieving goals. Regularly monitoring progress helps maintain accountability and motivation, promotes a positive mindset, and reinforces feelings of accomplishment. Tracking goals allows you to see your progress, which is a strong motivator to continue. This practice also helps identify obstacles early, enabling necessary adjustments (Harkin et al., 2016). Celebrating milestones releases dopamine, a neurotransmitter linked to pleasure and reward, enhancing overall well-being and encouraging further progress (*Celebrating Your Milestones*, 2023).

Methods for Tracking Progress

There are several effective methods for tracking your goals:

- **Journaling:** Keeping a journal allows you to reflect on your daily or weekly achievements and setbacks. This method helps you stay mindful of your progress and identify patterns needing adjustment.
- **Creating Charts:** Visual aids such as charts or graphs can be highly motivating. You can use spreadsheets to create bar charts, line graphs, or pie charts to visually represent your progress over time. This method is particularly useful for tracking numerical goals, like weight loss or financial savings.
- **Using Apps or Digital Tools:** Numerous apps designed to help you track your goals are available. Tools like Trello, Evernote, and dedicated goal-

tracking apps provide reminders, progress updates, and a visual overview of your achievements.
- **Setting Milestones or Checkpoints**: Breaking down larger goals into smaller, manageable milestones helps maintain motivation and provides regular opportunities to celebrate progress. This approach also makes it easier to adjust your plan as needed (Lim, 2020).

Celebrating Successes

Celebrating your successes is essential for maintaining motivation and reinforcing positive behaviors. Doing so helps you stay motivated and fosters a positive mindset that supports ongoing achievement. Here are some healthy and effective ways to celebrate your accomplishments:

- **Reward yourself**. Treat yourself to something special, like a favorite meal, a spa day, or a small gift. These rewards can serve as powerful incentives to keep you motivated.
- **Share achievements with others**. Sharing your successes with friends, family, or a support group can enhance your accomplishment and provide additional encouragement. Positive feedback from others reinforces your achievements and helps build a supportive community.
- **Reflect on lessons learned**. Reflect on what you did well and what you could improve. This reflection helps you appreciate your journey and apply any lessons learned to future goals.

- **Create a victory ritual.** Develop a personal ritual for celebrating milestones, such as lighting a candle, taking a hike, or writing a letter to yourself. These rituals can provide a sense of closure and satisfaction for each milestone achieved (Clarke, 2021).

Summary

- **Identifying Barriers to Success**: Understanding that self-limiting beliefs, negative thinking, fears, and self-sabotage behaviors are major obstacles is crucial. Recognizing these barriers is the first step in overcoming them, allowing you to move forward with a clearer path to success.
- **Cultivating a Growth Mindset and Self-Awareness**: Developing a growth mindset and increasing self-awareness are foundational approaches to breaking through these barriers. These strategies enable you to see challenges as growth opportunities and become more mindful of your thoughts and behaviors.
- **Prioritizing Self-Care**: Self-care is not just about indulgence: it involves nurturing your physical, emotional, mental, social, professional, financial, and spiritual well-being. Integrating self-care practices into your routine allows you to manage stress, build resilience, and maintain a positive outlook, all of which support personal growth and development.
- **Building a Supportive Network**: Surrounding yourself with a supportive network is essential. A strong support system helps reduce stress, improve

self-esteem, enhance resilience, and promote better health outcomes. Engage with family, friends, coworkers, and communities to create a robust support network.

- **Setting and Achieving Personal Goals**: Setting personal goals aligned with your core values and aspirations ensures they are meaningful and sustainable. Using the SMART criteria (Specific, Measurable, Achievable, Relevant, and Time-Bound) helps in systematically working toward these goals, tracking progress, and celebrating milestones, fostering continuous personal and professional growth.

Conclusion

Chapter 8 of *Transmute Your Mindset And Your Behind Will Follow* emphasized the importance of creating a supportive network and setting SMART goals. It provided practical strategies for building and maintaining a network that fosters growth and positivity. Additionally, the chapter discussed how setting SMART goals—specific, measurable, achievable, relevant, and time-bound—ensures clear and attainable objectives. These strategies aim to help you foster a positive environment and stay on track with your personal growth and mental well-being.

As we finish this book, let's see how each chapter connects to create a better mindset. We started with the basics of mental wellness. Reflective prompts and positive self-talk showed the power of our inner dialogue. We learned tools to change negative thoughts into positive ones. Self-compassion and mindfulness taught us to be kind to ourselves and stay present. Constructive feedback highlighted the value of a supportive network. Self-care strategies were discussed for maintaining well-being. Finally, setting SMART goals helped us create clear and achievable objectives.

All these elements aim to build a healthier, stronger mindset. Each chapter builds on the last, offering a layered approach to mental and emotional well-being. Managing your thoughts, building support systems, practicing self-care, and setting goals all work together to strengthen your mental health.

A Better Future

Congratulations on finishing *Transmute Your Mindset And Your Behind Will Follow*! You've shown a strong commitment to improving your mental and emotional health. The strategies and insights in this book give you tools to face life's challenges with resilience and optimism.

Remember, personal growth is a continuous journey. Each small step brings you closer to a better, more fulfilling future. Use the knowledge from this book to shape your life positively. Celebrate your progress and keep applying these strategies to maintain and enhance your well-being.

Thank you for letting this book be part of your journey. Here's to a brighter, healthier, and happier future!

You Can Help Someone Else Be Their Best Self

In the second half of this book, you have seen how you can often be your worst enemy—especially when you let self-sabotaging thoughts take over. By embracing the growth mindset, you can use every single setback as an opportunity to know yourself and others better—and to fine-tune your communication, planning, leadership, and so many other skills.

You have also seen that you never stop growing, discovering who you are, and occasionally, making mistakes—but that's good, too, as it enables you to continue developing into who you want to be. Let others know that they can create a brighter future for themselves, simply by adopting a flexible mindset.

WANT TO HELP OTHERS?

Show new readers that they can change their lives for the better by simply using their minds in the right way.

Click the link or scan the QR code to leave your review on Amazon:

https://www.amazon.com/review/create-review/?asin=B0DG86N7QB

Conclusion

As we wrap up *Transmute Your Mindset And Your Behind Will Follow*, one surprising fact stands out: our mindset affects every part of our lives. Whether we see our abilities as fixed or capable of growth makes a huge difference. Through this book, I hope I have shown you how adopting a growth mindset can lead to big changes in your personal and professional life.

Reflecting back to the beginning of this book, remember the personal story about letting go of a relationship that wasn't working. Despite the fear, that decision to embrace change and growth paved the way for a happier and healthier life. My journey exemplifies the core message of this book: by changing our mindset and embracing growth, we can transform our lives. Once you learn how to change your mind, everything else will follow.

Together, we've looked at how powerful reflective prompts and positive self-talk can be. Our internal dialogue shapes our reality. Tools like cognitive restructuring and thought records can help you turn negative thoughts into positive ones. At the same time, learning self-compassion and mindfulness helps us be kinder to ourselves and stay focused on the present. We've also seen the importance of having a supportive network and giving and receiving constructive feedback from your trusted circle. These help us create a positive environment and set clear, achievable objectives that keep us motivated and on track.

You might still struggle with self-sabotage and limiting beliefs, but you have learned that these often come from past experiences and societal norms. Know that by identifying and challenging these beliefs and using positive affirmations, we can break free and reach our full potential. Your awareness is a vital first step.

The main message from this book is that growth and improvement are within each of us. By adopting a growth mindset, challenging limiting beliefs, and creating supportive habits, we can overcome obstacles. Personal growth is a journey, not a destination. Every step, no matter how small, brings us closer to a fulfilled and confident life. Celebrate your progress, use these strategies, and look forward to a brighter, healthier, and happier future.

Have faith in your ability to shape the life you desire. You have the inner strength to overcome challenges, achieve your goals, and live a fulfilling and purposeful life. Trust yourself and know you can face any obstacle with confidence and determination. Keep moving forward, always believing in your potential and the incredible journey ahead. With this mindset, you can turn your dreams into reality and create a life that aligns with your aspirations and passions.

If you found value in this book, please consider leaving a review. Your feedback helps me improve my work and guides others on their personal growth and fulfillment journeys. By sharing your thoughts, you can help others discover the insights and strategies that have made a difference in your life. Your review can inspire and empower someone else to take the first step toward creating the life they desire.

Thank you for letting this book be part of your journey. Remember, when you free your mind, your actions will follow. By "freeing your mind," I mean letting go of limiting beliefs, negative self-talk, and fixed mindsets that hold you back. When your mind is free, your actions naturally align with this newfound freedom and positivity. Here's to unlocking your true potential and embracing the limitless possibilities ahead.

References

5 Ways to Get Mindfulness into Your Everyday Life. (n.d.). Headspace. https://www.headspace.com/articles/5-ways-to-get-mindfulness-into-your-everyday-life

7 Easy Ways to Be Mindful in Your Everyday Life. (n.d.). Happify. https://www.happify.com/hd/7-ways-to-be-mindful-in-your-everyday-life/

10 Feedback Styles with Examples of How to Use Them. (2022). Indeed. https://www.indeed.com/career-advice/career-development/feedback-styles

10 Limiting Beliefs and How to Overcome Them. (2021, November 29). Asana. https://asana.com/resources/limiting-beliefs

13 Common Limiting Beliefs Holding Us Back. (2023, December 31). Career Contessa. https://www.careercontessa.com/advice/limiting-beliefs/

80 Common Limiting Beliefs Examples That Are Holding You Back. (2021, December 23). Joyful through It All. https://www.joyfulthroughitall.com/limiting-beliefs-examples/

Ackerman, C. E. (2018, July 5). *Positive Mindset: How to Develop a Positive Mental Attitude*. PositivePsychology.com. https://positivepsychology.com/positive-mindset/#traits-positive-mindset

Adrian, J. (2020, July 9). *Why Mindset Matters in Relationships*. Medium. https://jonathanoei.medium.com/why-mindset-matters-in-relationships-614c8b98fb99

Agrawal, M. (2023, April 25). *"Why Mindset Matters for Personal Development."* LinkedIn. https://www.linkedin.com/pulse/why-mindset-matters-personal-development-mohit-agrawal/

Allemand, H. (2023, March 10). *The Power of Mindset: How Your Attitude Can Impact Your Career Success*. LinkedIn. https://www.linkedin.com/pulse/power-mindset-how-your-attitude-can-impact-career-success-allemand/

Anthony, P. (2016, October 5). *Reframe Fear to Overcome Fear*. UGN Automotive. https://ugn.com/reframe-fear-to-overcome-fear/

Ashbridge, Z. (2023, June 14). *How to Develop a Support System for Better Mental health*. GoDaddy Blog. https://www.godaddy.com/resources/mindset/how-to-develop-a-support-system-for-better-mental-health

Ballesteros, R. (2018, September 2). *Why Self Awareness and the Growth Mindset Can 10x Your Success in Life*. Ascent Publication. https://medium.

com/the-ascent/why-self-awareness-and-the-growth-mindset-can-10x-your-success-in-life-471c692c6e8a#:

Brooten-Brooks, M. (2022, May 23). *What Is Self-Compassion?* Verywell Health. https://www.verywellhealth.com/self-compassion-5220012#toc-how-to-practice-self-compassion-8-life-changing-techniques

Build a Support System with a Great Network of People. (2020, February 13). University of the People. https://www.uopeople.edu/blog/what-is-a-support-system/

Carol Dweck: Thinker. (n.d.). The Decision Lab. https://thedecisionlab.com/thinkers/psychology/carol-dweck

Casabianca, S. S. (2021, May 6). *15 Cognitive Distortions to Blame for Your Negative Thinking.* Psych Central. https://psychcentral.com/lib/cognitive-distortions-negative-thinking#polarization

Celebrating Your Milestones: Unlocking the Motivational Power of Progress. (2023, June 30). WindowStill. https://www.windowstill.com/celebrating-your-milestones-unlocking-the-motivational-power-of-progress/posts/#:

Cherry, K. (2021, April 8). *Mindfulness Meditation.* Verywell Mind. https://www.verywellmind.com/mindfulness-meditation-88369

Cherry, K. (2022a, September 20). *Why Cultivating a Growth Mindset Can Boost Your Success.* Verywell Mind. https://www.verywellmind.com/what-is-a-mindset-2795025#toc-what-is-a-mindset

Cherry, K. (2022b, November 8). *What Is Neuroplasticity?* Verywell Mind. https://www.verywellmind.com/what-is-brain-plasticity-2794886

Cherry, K. (2022c, November 14). *What Is Procrastination?* Verywell Mind. https://www.verywellmind.com/the-psychology-of-procrastination-2795944#toc-how-to-overcome-procrastination

Cherry, K. (2023a, January 20). *What Is the Fear of Success?* Verywell Mind. https://www.verywellmind.com/what-is-the-fear-of-success-5179184#:

Cherry, K. (2023b, March 3). *A Social Support System Is Imperative for Health and Well-Being.* Verywell Mind. https://www.verywellmind.com/social-support-for-psychological-health-4119970#toc-health-benefits-of-social-support

Clarke, J. (2021, October 7). *Boost Confidence and Connections by Celebrating Success the Right Way.* Verywell Mind. https://www.verywellmind.com/healthy-ways-to-celebrate-success-4163887

Coelho, S., & Smith, J. (2013, June 13). *Benefits of Self-Compassion: 7 Benefits and How to Practice.* Psych Central. https://psychcentral.com/blog/practicing-self-compassion-when-you-have-a-mental-illness#growth-mindset

Cox, J. (2022, November 15). *7 Ways to Cope with Perfectionism*. Psych Central. https://psychcentral.com/health/steps-to-conquer-perfectionism

Cuncic, A. (2022, November 17). *Imposter Syndrome: Why You May Feel Like a Fraud*. Verywell Mind. https://www.verywellmind.com/imposter-syndrome-and-social-anxiety-disorder-4156469

Cuncic, A. (2023, August 30). *Simple Steps to Start Practicing Guided Imagery for Anxiety Relief*. Verywell Mind. https://www.verywellmind.com/how-do-you-practice-guided-imagery-for-anxiety-3024396

Davis, T. (n.d.). *Mindsets: Definition, Examples, and Books (Growth, Fixed + Other Types)*. The Berkeley Well-Being Institute. Retrieved March 10, 2024, from https://www.berkeleywellbeing.com/mindsets.html#:

Davis, T. (2019, April 11). *15 Ways to Build a Growth Mindset*. Psychology Today. https://www.psychologytoday.com/us/blog/click-here-happiness/201904/15-ways-build-growth-mindset

Deep breathing exercise. (2016). Torbay and South Devon NHS Foundation Trust. https://www.torbayandsouthdevon.nhs.uk/services/pain-service/reconnect2life/creating-skills-for-the-future/learning-relaxation-skills/deep-breathing-exercise/

DeFranzo, S. E. (2018, July 31). *5 Reasons Why Feedback Is Important*. Snap Surveys Blog. https://www.snapsurveys.com/blog/5-reasons-feedback-important/

Delves, R. (2020, February 11). *Do You Suffer from Imposter Syndrome? Identify and Manage Your Inner Negative Voice*. Hult International Business School. https://www.hult.edu/blog/do-you-suffer-from-imposter-syndrome-identify-and-manage-your-inner-negative-voice/

Dempsey, L. (2023, March 6). *Three Benefits of Self-Awareness*. Nebraska Methodist Health System. https://bestcareeap.org/resource-hub/three-benefits-self-awareness

Developing Your Support System. (n.d.). University at Buffalo School of Social Work. https://socialwork.buffalo.edu/resources/self-care-starter-kit/additional-self-care-resources/developing-your-support-system.html

Dorwart, L. (2023, September 19). *Understanding the Psychology Behind Perfectionism*. Verywell Health. https://www.verywellhealth.com/perfectionism-5323816#toc-definition-of-perfectionism

Durden, T. (2021, September 8). *7 Factors That Influence Your Mindset*. Fearless Business Boss. https://fearlessbusinessboss.com/7-factors-that-influence-your-mindset/

Effect of Negative Thinking: Meaning & Causes. (n.d.). Digit Insurance. https://

www.godigit.com/health-insurance/mental-health/effect-of-negative-thinking

Fargo, S. (2016, June 13). *Breath Awareness Meditation*. Mindfulness Exercises. https://mindfulnessexercises.com/breath-awareness-meditation/

Fear. (2022). Dictionary of Psychology. https://dictionary.apa.org/fear

Fear of Failure (Atychiphobia): Causes & Treatment. (n.d.). Cleveland Clinic. Retrieved April 10, 2024, from https://my.clevelandclinic.org/health/diseases/22555-atychiphobia-fear-of-failure#symptoms-and-causes

Field, B. (2023, November 3). *Why We Self-Sabotage and How To Stop the Cycle*. Verywell Mind. https://www.verywellmind.com/why-people-self-sabotage-and-how-to-stop-it-5207635#toc-what-causes-self-sabotaging-behavior

Fixed Mindset. (2023). The Decision Lab. https://thedecisionlab.com/reference-guide/psychology/fixed-mindset

Fixed Mindset vs. Growth Mindset: Differences and Examples. (2022, August 8). Indeed Career Guide. https://www.indeed.com/career-advice/career-development/fixed-vs-growth-mindset

Fixed Mindset: Definition, Pros & Cons, Examples & Comparison. (2021, August 26). HIGH5 TEST. https://high5test.com/fixed-mindset/

Fletcher, J. (2019, February 12). *4-7-8 Breathing: How It Works, Benefits, and Uses*. Medical News Today. https://www.medicalnewstoday.com/articles/324417

Foy, C. (2023, October 14). *Rational vs. Irrational Fears? How to Tell the Difference*. FHE Health. https://fherehab.com/learning/rational-irrational-fears

French, M. (2023, October 19). *Self-Sabotage: How to Overcome Self-Defeating Behavior*. Medical News Today. https://www.medicalnewstoday.com/articles/self-sabotage#causes

Garey, J. (n.d.). *How to Change Negative Thinking Patterns*. Child Mind Institute. Retrieved April 6, 2024, from https://childmind.org/article/how-to-change-negative-thinking-patterns/#1-all-or-nothing-thinking-also-referred-to-as-black-and-white-thinking-or-dichotomous-thinking

Goal Setting for Success: Empower Yourself to Set and Achieve Goals. (2024, May 23). Gray Group International. https://www.graygroupintl.com/blog/goal-setting-for-success#:

Goldman, R. (2022, November 4). *Affirmations: What They Are and How to Use Them*. Everyday Health. https://www.everydayhealth.com/emotional-health/what-are-affirmations/

Graham, K. (2018, October 16). *Mindset Matters: How Your Thoughts Affect Your*

Health. Ace Fitness https://www.acefitness.org/resources/everyone/blog/7119/mindset-matters-how-your-thoughts-affect-your-health/

Harkin, B., Webb, T. L., Chang, B. P. I., Prestwich, A., Conner, M., Kellar, I., Benn, Y., & Sheeran, P. (2016). Does Monitoring Goal Progress Promote Goal Attainment? A Meta-Analysis of the Experimental Evidence. *Psychological Bulletin, 142*(2), 198–229. https://doi.org/10.1037/bul0000025

Harper, C. (n.d.). *How to Build a Support System for Your Mental Health*. MyWellbeing. https://mywellbeing.com/therapy-101/how-to-build-a-support-system

Ho, L. (2020, February 5). *20 Personal SMART Goals Examples to Improve Your Life*. Lifehack. https://www.lifehack.org/864427/examples-of-personal-smart-goals

Hoshaw, C. (2022, March 29). *What Mindfulness Really Means and How to Practice*. Healthline. https://www.healthline.com/health/mind-body/what-is-mindfulness#mindful-therapy

How Does Mindset Impact Personal Growth? (n.d.). Selfpause. Retrieved March 23, 2024, from https://selfpause.com/mindset/how-does-mindset-impact-personal-growth/

How Does Mindset Impact Relationships? (n.d.). Selfpause. Retrieved March 23, 2024, from https://selfpause.com/mindset/how-does-mindset-impact-relationships/

How Does Mindset Impact Self-Awareness? (n.d.). Selfpause. Retrieved May 14, 2024, from https://selfpause.com/mindset/how-does-mindset-impact-self-awareness/

How Does Negative Thinking Affect Your Social Skills? (2022, August 25). The Social Skills Center. https://socialskillscenter.com/how-does-negative-thinking-affect-your-social-skills/

How to Change Your Mindset: 5 Ways to Change Your Mindset. (2022, December 1). MasterClass. https://www.masterclass.com/articles/how-to-change-your-mindset

How To Practice Mindfulness Meditation. (2018, November 27). Mindful. https://www.mindful.org/mindfulness-how-to-do-it/

How to Receive Feedback with a Growth Mindset. (2019, August). NeuroLeadership Institute. https://neuroleadership.com/your-brain-at-work/receive-feedback-with-growth-mindset/

Hyatt, M. (2014, October 6). *How to Reframe Your Fear and Let It Work for You*. Full Focus. https://fullfocus.co/reframe-fear/

Impostor Syndrome: What It Is and How to Overcome It. (2022, April 4).

References

Cleveland Clinic. https://health.clevelandclinic.org/a-psychologist-explains-how-to-deal-with-imposter-syndrome

Ionescu, I. (2021, April 6). *Why You Should Always Align Your Goals and Values*. Iulian Ionescu. https://iulianionescu.com/blog/align-your-goals-and-values/

Jewell, M. (n.d.). *Align Your Goals with Your Values*. Selling Energy. https://www.sellingenergy.com/blog/align-your-goals-with-your-values

Johnson, C. (2020, May 18). *How Mindset Is Formed From Childhood*. CHALENE JOHNSON. https://chalene.com/how-mindset-is-formed/

Johnson, D. (2023, March 3). *What Is the Difference Between Beliefs and Attitudes?* Similar Different. https://similardifferent.com/difference-between-beliefs-and-attitudes/

Johnson, J. (2020, May 27). *What Is Diaphragmatic Breathing? Benefits and How-To*. Medical News Today. https://www.medicalnewstoday.com/articles/diaphragmatic-breathing#how-to-do-it

Kachigan, M. (2021, October 7). *Limiting Beliefs - How Those Are Holding You Back & How To Change*. Official Teamly Blog. https://www.teamly.com/blog/limiting-beliefs/#what_effects_do_limiting_beliefs_have_on_a_person_or_team

Kristenson, S. (2023a, April 5). *21 Limiting Beliefs Examples That Hold You Back in Life*. Happier Human. https://www.happierhuman.com/limiting-beliefs/

Kristenson, S. (2023b, April 6). *10 Growth Mindset Goals Examples to Change Your Thinking*. Develop Good Habits. https://www.developgoodhabits.com/growth-mindset-goals-wa1/

Ladouceur, C. (n.d.). *Practice Self-Compassion to Protect Against Self-Sabotage*. Coach Chrystal's Eat Move Live. Retrieved April 22, 2024, from https://coachchrystal.ca/practice-self-compassion-to-protect-against-self-sabotage/

Legg, T. (2016, December 19). *Self-Talk: Why It Matters*. Healthline. https://www.healthline.com/health/mental-health/self-talk#how-does-it-work

Leikvoll, V. (2022, September 6). *20 Life-Changing Personal Development Goals*. Leaders. https://leaders.com/articles/personal-growth/personal-development-goals/

Lim, S. (2020, April 21). *How to Track Your Goals: 5 Fabulous Ways You Should Consider*. Stunning Motivation. https://stunningmotivation.com/track-your-goals/

Logie, J. (2020). *3 Ways a Negative Mindset Is Ruining Your Life & How to Beat It - Learning Mind*. Learning Mind. https://www.learning-mind.com/negative-mindset-beat/

Luna, A. (2018, September 10). *Do You Suffer From the Fear of Rejection? (Read These 9 Inspiring Tips).* LonerWolf. https://lonerwolf.com/fear-of-rejection/#h-what-is-the-fear-of-rejection

Mastering Love: How A Growth Mindset Helps You Adapt To Relationship Challenges. (2023, November 13). Dateworks. https://www.dateworks.co/blog/mastering-love-how-a-growth-mindset-helps-you-adapt-to-relationship-challenges/#:

Matthews, D. (2020, January 9). *How to Identify Your Limiting Beliefs and Get Over Them.* Lifehack. https://www.lifehack.org/858652/limiting-beliefs#causes-of-limiting-beliefs

McD, K. (2020, December 21). *Journaling for Self-Awareness: 6 Reasons to Journal.* My Question Life. https://myquestionlife.com/journaling-for-self-awareness/

McLeod, L. (2015, December 4). *This Is How You Give Honest Feedback to Anyone, Anytime—Without Hurting Feelings.* The Muse. https://www.themuse.com/advice/this-is-how-you-give-honest-feedback-to-anyone-anytimewithout-hurting-feelings

Meier, J. D. (n.d.). *What Is a Mindset?* Sources of Insight. https://sourcesofinsight.com/what-is-mindset/#whatisamindset

Mether, L. (2018, September 3). *Boost Your Self-Awareness with Personal Feedback.* Leah Mether. https://www.leahmether.com.au/boost-self-awareness-constructive-feedback/

Migala, J. (2023, August 20). *Quick Stretches for Stress Relief You Can Do Right Now.* Everyday Health. https://www.everydayhealth.com/fitness/quick-stretches-for-stress-relief/

Mindfulness. (n.d.). Psychology Today. https://www.psychologytoday.com/us/basics/mindfulness#the-benefits-of-mindfulness

Mindset Matters: Abundance Mindset vs. Scarcity Mindset. (n.d.). The Strategic Coach Inc. https://resources.strategiccoach.com/the-multiplier-mindset-blog/mindset-matters-abundance-mindset-vs-scarcity-mindset

Moore, C. (2019, June 2). *How to Practice Self-Compassion: 8 Techniques and Tips.* PositivePsychology.com. https://positivepsychology.com/how-to-practice-self-compassion/#8-tips-and-techniques-for-practicing-self-compassion

Negative Thought Patterns and Depression. (2022, January 11). Maryland Recovery. https://www.marylandrecovery.com/blog/overcoming-negative-thinking-patterns#:

Newlyn, E. (2022, October 10). *How to Change Your Mind - The Power of*

Neuroplasticity. Ekhart Yoga. https://www.ekhartyoga.com/articles/practice/how-to-change-your-mind-the-power-of-neuroplasticity

O'Shea, D. (n.d.). *5 Advantages of Having a Strong Support System*. Www.droshea.com. https://www.droshea.com/blog/you-are-not-an-island

Pasha, R. (2017, February 8). *Limiting Beliefs: How to Identify and Overcome Them*. Succeed Feed. https://succeedfeed.com/limiting-beliefs/#:

Peer, M. (2020, August 7). *Fear of Rejection: Its Origin, Effects, and How To Overcome It*. Marisa Peer. https://marisapeer.com/fear-of-rejection/

Perry, E. (2022, March 17). *You Are Your Only Obstacle: Learn How to Overcome Self Sabotage*. BetterUp. https://www.betterup.com/blog/self-sabotage#:

Perry, E. (2023a, May 8). *How to Set Goals and Achieve Them: 10 Strategies for Success*. BetterUp. https://www.betterup.com/blog/how-to-set-goals-and-achieve-them#how-to-set-achievable-goals-at-work-and-in-life%C2%A0

Perry, E. (2023b, December 4). *How to Stop Being a People-Pleaser and Regain Your Freedom*. BetterUp. https://www.betterup.com/blog/how-to-stop-being-a-people-pleaser

Peterson, T. J. (2023, March 6). *Fear of Failure: Causes & 5 Ways to Cope with Atychiphobia*. Choosing Therapy. https://www.choosingtherapy.com/fear-of-failure/

Picardi, L. (2022, June 12). *How to Effectively Write Affirmations and Practice Them + Examples*. Gratitude - The Life Blog. https://blog.gratefulness.me/how-to-write-affirmations-how-to-do-affirmations/#:

Pietrangelo, A. (2020, September 30). *What Is a Fear of Success?* Healthline. https://www.healthline.com/health/anxiety/fear-of-success#what-it-looks-like

Pradeepa, S. (2022, November 24). *Attitude and Mindset: Intersection, Importance, & Difference*. Believe in Mind. https://www.believeinmind.com/self-growth/attitude-and-mindset-how-do-they-differ/#htoc-are-attitude-and-mindset-the-same-thing

Pradeepa, S. (2023a, April 9). *30 Abundance Mindset Examples: Practice Abundance Now*. Believe in Mind. https://www.believeinmind.com/mindset/abundance-mindset-examples/

Pradeepa, S. (2023b, May 8). *31 Scarcity Mindset Examples: What Everybody Ought to Know*. Believe in Mind. https://www.believeinmind.com/mindset/scarcity-mindset-examples/

Primeau, M. (2021, September 15). *Your Powerful, Changeable Mindset*. Stanford Report. https://news.stanford.edu/report/2021/09/15/mindsets-clearing-lens-life/#:

Ratcliffe, S. (Ed.). (2016). *Oxford Essential Quotations* (4th ed.). Oxford

University Press. https://www.oxfordreference.com/display/10.1093/acref/9780191826719.001.0001/q-oro-ed4-00003960#:

Ravelo, L. (2021, November 26). *Why Are Goals Important? 18 Reasons Why and More*. Creativity Mesh. https://creativitymesh.com/why-are-goals-important/

Raypole, C. (2020, March 26). *Body Scan Meditation: Benefits and How to Do It*. Healthline. https://www.healthline.com/health/body-scan-meditation#how-to-do-it

Raypole, C. (2022, February 28). *How Many Thoughts Do You Have Per Day? And Other FAQs*. Healthline. https://www.healthline.com/health/how-many-thoughts-per-day#thoughts-per-day

Receiving and Giving Effective Feedback. (2019). Centre for Teaching Excellence. https://uwaterloo.ca/centre-for-teaching-excellence/catalogs/tip-sheets/receiving-and-giving-effective-feedback

Riani, A. (2023, May 31). *Drawing Inspiration from Thomas Edison: 3 Essential Lessons for Startup Founders*. Forbes. https://www.forbes.com/sites/abdoriani/2023/05/31/drawing-inspiration-from-thomas-edison-3-essential-lessons-for-startup-founders/?sh=43b96662ae84

Richardson, C. (2022, April 28). *Body scan meditation: How to Do It and Benefits*. Medical News Today. https://www.medicalnewstoday.com/articles/body-scan-meditation#how-to-do-it

Rozen, M. (n.d.). *Why Fear of Success Is More Powerful than Fear of Failure*. Drmichellerozen.com. https://www.drmichellerozen.com/executive-coaching/fear-of-success-vs-fear-of-failure/

Saab, L., & Javanbakht, A. (2017, October 27). *What Happens in the Brain When We Feel Fear*. Smithsonian. https://www.smithsonianmag.com/science-nature/what-happens-brain-feel-fear-180966992/

Saymeh, A. (2023, February 22). *What Is Imposter Syndrome? Definition, Symptoms, and Overcoming It*. BetterUp. https://www.betterup.com/blog/what-is-imposter-syndrome-and-how-to-avoid-it

Scott, E. (2019). *How to Make Mindfulness Your Way of Life*. Verywell Mind. https://www.verywellmind.com/mindfulness-exercises-for-everyday-life-3145187

Self-Sabotaging: Why We Do It & 8 Ways to Stop. (2023, September 28). Choosing Therapy, Inc. https://www.choosingtherapy.com/self-sabotaging/#examples-of-self-sabotaging-behavior

Self-talk. (2022, March 4). Healthdirect Australia. https://www.healthdirect.gov.au/self-talk#tips-negative

Smith, E.-M. (2022, March 25). *What Is Negative Thinking? How It Destroys*

Your Mental Health. Healthy Place. https://www.healthyplace.com/self-help/positivity/what-is-negative-thinking-how-it-destroys-your-mental-health

Smith, M., Robinson, L., & Segal, J. (2019, May 7). *Phobias and Irrational Fears*. HelpGuide.org. https://www.helpguide.org/articles/anxiety/phobias-and-irrational-fears.htm

Soken-Huberty, E. (2023, July 21). *10 Reasons Why Self-Awareness Is Important*. Open Education Online. https://openeducationonline.com/magazine/10-reasons-why-self-awareness-is-important/

Spacey, J. (2020, September 13). *19 Examples of Mindset*. Simplicable. https://simplicable.com/philosophy/mindset

Sparks, S. D. (2021, April 9). *"Growth Mindset" Linked to Higher Test Scores, Student Well-Being in Global Study*. Education Week. https://www.edweek.org/leadership/growth-mindset-linked-to-higher-test-scores-student-well-being-in-global-study/2021/04

Stanborough, R. J. (2020, February 4). *How to Change Negative Thinking with Cognitive Restructuring*. Healthline. https://www.healthline.com/health/cognitive-restructuring

Talesnik, D. (2019, June 28). *Eurich Explores Why Self-Awareness Matters*. NIH Record. https://nihrecord.nih.gov/2019/06/28/eurich-explores-why-self-awareness-matters

Tallon, M. (2020, April 13). *10 Simple Ways to Practice Mindfulness in Our Daily Life*. Monique Tallon. https://moniquetallon.com/10-simple-ways-to-practice-mindfulness-in-our-daily-life/

Tanasugarn, A. (2022, September 25). *How Negative Self-Beliefs Can Impact Your Life*. Psychology Today. https://www.psychologytoday.com/intl/blog/understanding-ptsd/202209/how-negative-self-beliefs-can-impact-your-life

Tartakovsky, M. (2022, February 22). *15 Benefits of Journaling and Tips for Getting Started*. Healthline. https://www.healthline.com/health/benefits-of-journaling

The Power of Mindset and Goal Setting. (2023, June 16). Key of Mindset. https://keyofmindset.com/the-power-of-mindset-and-goal-setting/#:

Vallejo, M. (2023, September 6). *Negative Thinking Patterns: Common Types and How to Overcome Them*. Mental Health Center Kids. https://mentalhealthcenterkids.com/blogs/articles/negative-thinking-patterns#what-are-negative-thinking-patterns

Van Edwards, V. (2021, January 11). *10 Powerful Tips You Can Use to Practice Self-Compassion*. Science of People. https://www.scienceofpeople.com/self-compassion/#what-is-self-compassion

Van Horn, H. (2023, August 9). *Limiting Beliefs: How They Hold You Back and*

How to Break Free. Day One Your Journal for Life. https://dayoneapp.com/blog/limiting-beliefs/#h-the-impact-of-limited-beliefs

Vermeer, A. (2012 February). *Mindsets: Where do they come from?* Alexvermeer.com. https://alexvermeer.com/mindsets-where-do-they-come-from/#:

Walichowski, M. (2018, January 9). *Journal to Increase Your Growth Mindset and Grit*. MiraNous. https://miranous.com/journal-increase-growth-mindset-grit/

Why You Procrastinate and How to Stop. (2022, February 22). Cleveland Clinic. https://health.clevelandclinic.org/how-to-stop-procrastinating

Wiebe, J. (2019, April 10). *5 Ways to Strengthen Your Support System*. Talkspace. https://www.talkspace.com/blog/how-to-strengthen-your-support-system/

Winch, G. (2013, June 18). *10 Signs that You Might Have Fear of Failure*. Psychology Today. https://www.psychologytoday.com/intl/blog/the-squeaky-wheel/201306/10-signs-that-you-might-have-fear-of-failure

Wooll, M. (2021, July 26). *13 Tips to Develop a Growth Mindset*. BetterUp. https://www.betterup.com/blog/growth-mindset#

Wooll, M. (2022a, June 28). *15 Goals for Self-Improvement (Plus, Tips to Achieve Them)*. BetterUp. https://www.betterup.com/blog/goals-for-self-improvement

Wooll, M. (2022b, July 19). *Don't Let Limiting Beliefs Hold You Back. Learn to Overcome Yours*. BetterUp. https://www.betterup.com/blog/what-are-limiting-beliefs

Wooll, M. (2022c, July 19). *What Are Limiting Beliefs*. BetterUp. https://www.betterup.com/blog/what-are-limiting-beliefs#:

Yugay, I. (2022, August 17). *How Limiting Beliefs Might Be Holding You Back & How to Fix Them*. Mindvalley Blog. https://blog.mindvalley.com/limiting-beliefs/#h-how-to-identify-limiting-beliefs

Zorbas, A. (2023, June 12). *The Power of Cognitive Restructuring: Reframing Your Thoughts for a Healthier Mindset*. Therapy Now. https://www.therapynowsf.com/blog/the-power-of-cognitive-restructuring-reframing-your-thoughts-for-a-healthier-mindset/d/RismDHDiFxJr2e709bas

www.ingramcontent.com/pod-product-compliance
Lightning Source LLC
Chambersburg PA
CBHW070624030426
42337CB00020B/3909